To Pa[illegible]

Many t[illegible]

and your family,

Fondly,

Pam Ferriss

Susan Kelton

Kathy Maul

KATHRYN MARCH PAMELA FERRISS SUSAN KELTON

My Grandmother is...

praying for me

daily prayers and proverbs for character development in grandchildren

First Edition

Cover and Interior Design by Don Wise Productions, Inc.
Edited by Anne Severance

My Grandmother Is, LLC
www.mygrandmotheris.com
P.O. Box 3126, Brentwood, TN 37024

ISBN 978-0-9774424-3-0

13 12 11 10 09 / 5 4 3 2 1

For all our grandchildren

May the Lord richly bless you
through the faithful prayers
of your parents and grandparents.

Contents

Foreword

Standard wisdom for families on road trips has been that the wife had better pack a map, because no self-respecting man would ever stop and ask directions. However lost he may become, whatever hours are added to the trip trying to weave his way back onto the right route, a true man's man is simply not interested in anyone's imposition of directions.

All this changed with the advent of the GPS. This is not merely because maps are becoming obsolete with the dawn of this new technology, but simply because men love consumer electronics! Now, men are more than willing to confess their directional ineptitude, if only *she* will permit him to go to the electronics store and buy a GPS.

Truth is, we are all directionally challenged. Sin clouds our vision, and our idolatrous hearts want to carve out paths of our own choosing. Yet God is faithful. He has not left us without a map, the lines of which trace the trajectory of redemption from a dignified beginning in a paradisiacal garden, to the fallout of the Fall, to a cross and a tomb—neither of which could hold down the Redeeming Mapmaker—all the way to a consummate beginning in a new heaven and earth. And right in the middle of that story, a trove of wisdom for the journey for those of us who live amidst the fallout of that Fall, between redemption and consummation.

Wisdom has been a hot commodity in various cultures throughout human history. One need not search far to find collections of wise maxims tuned for keeping one from folly. A quick web search turns up Irish proverbs, English proverbs, Chinese proverbs, African proverbs... a proverbial cornucopia of wise words. And there is much wisdom to be mined in many of these sources. God, in His common grace to human beings created in His image, has allowed the discovery of certain truths, even among those who do not acknowledge the source of truth. The assumption, whatever the culture, whatever the epoch in human history, is that the wise person will take the wisdom and run with it—live it out.

Something more is needed...some *One* more is needed. This is why the biblical proverbs cannot be summarily tossed onto the generic pile of wisdom this world has to offer. To think of the biblical Proverbs as mere good advice, is like calling a Stradivarius a fiddle. Indeed, Proverbs in the Bible is not given so we can hear wise advice and run with it, but ultimately that we might *run to and with* the source of wisdom, Christ Jesus, who has become for us "wisdom from God—and righteousness and sanctification and redemption" (1Corinthians 1:30, NKJB).

So, when we call our loved ones, our brothers and sisters in Christ, our children and grandchildren, and ourselves to live out the wisdom of Proverbs, we are doing more than suggesting moralistic, outward conformity. We are calling them to lean into Christ, who has become for us wisdom, because we are bereft of it in and of ourselves. Let us remind our grandchildren that it is not wise living that merits God's saving grace, but rather that living wisely is the joyful response to God's saving grace at work in our lives. And when they act foolishly, when they fail to live with integrity, generosity, etc., they shall not despair, for they have One who has become wisdom from God, *and righteousness and sanctification and redemption*, and so they may cling to Him in their weakness. We must teach our grandchildren that the pursuit of wisdom and integrity is a hopeful process even when they stumble, because they are united to Christ. Wisdom is not some thing way out there, foreign, hard to access, impossible to imitate. Wisdom is theirs as they learn of, live for, and love the Lord Jesus. Calling them to wisdom is simply calling them to be disciples (which word in the Greek means *learners*) of Christ.

To pray for our grandchildren's growth in character development is a uniquely Christ-like thing to do. Jesus prays similarly for believers in his High Priestly prayer, when he asks His Father, "Sanctify them in the truth; your word is truth" (John 17:7). You see, to pray that our grandchildren will live according to Proverbs or any other part of that toolbox of sanctification that is the Bible, is to pray for their growth in holiness and conformity to Christ (see Romans 8:28-29). Sanctification is a certainty (see Romans 8:30), for the God who causes our salvation, carries our salvation and completes our salvation, as Paul says, "Being confident of this, that he who began a good work in you will carry it on to completion until the day of Jesus Christ" (Philippians 1:6).

Though your prayers be weak and inconsistent at times, though your own pursuit of wisdom may not always be exemplary, though your grandchildren ebb and flow in their interest in being wise, take great comfort in knowing that no one, not even you, is more committed to the sanctification of covenant children than God Himself. So, teach them wisdom, pray for them, and remind them that they and you, empowered by Christ (see Colossians 1:29), "can do all things through Him who strengthens [you]" (Philippians 4:13).

Pray with the aid of this little book that these three

grandmothers have written. Think of it as a GPS unit of sorts—a "Grandparents' Prayer System"—as you seek to love and lead your little ones in biblical wisdom. For to pray for our grandchildren that they would learn and live out the principles of the Book of Proverbs is itself an act of obedience to Scripture: "If any of you lacks wisdom, he should ask God, who gives generously to all without finding fault, and it will be given him" (James 1:5).

Did you catch that? Yes, it is God who gives wisdom. But are you ready to believe in His generosity in giving? Are you ready to believe that He does not reproach you for your own lack of wisdom or your grandchildren for their occasional forays into folly? He will, with integrity and perfect timing, supply your needs and theirs. So, go on, ask in faith and don't doubt (James 1:6). As John Newton has taught us to sing:

Thou art coming to a King,
Large petitions with thee bring;
For his grace and power are such
None can ever ask too much.

--David Owen Filson, Pastor
Good Shepherd Presbyterian Church
Nashville, Tennessee
(For an expanded treatment by Pastor Filson of Proverbs, please see our website, www.mygrandmotheris.com)

Introduction

If you are reading this book, you are most likely a grandmother. Or maybe you know a grandmother, are married to one, or fondly remember your own. Whatever the case, we invite you to join us in getting involved in the lives of grandchildren. God has placed in our hearts the passion to pray for the next generation to become men and women of strong character and great faith.

Over a year ago, the three of us—Kathy, Pam, and Susan—sat down together to consider how God could use us in the lives of our grandchildren. We were all relatively new at grandmothering, but each had the same vision—to pass on a legacy of genuine faith, much like the description in 2 Timothy 1:5: "I have been reminded of your sincere faith which first lived in your grandmother Lois and in your mother Eunice."

Like so many grandparents today, we don't live near most of our grandchildren, so interacting with them frequently isn't possible. Yet we all desired to have a daily influence on these young ones who are so dear to our hearts. We decided this could be accomplished through intentional prayer. Thus, the idea of a daily devotional prayer book specifically for grandmothers was birthed.

The story of this book actually began earlier when the Lord led one of the authors to pray through the book of Proverbs for the character development of her grandchildren. As the three of us discussed this practice and studied this great book of wisdom, we realized that while the verses contain directives by which to live, these alone cannot produce godly character. It is ultimately the quickening of God's Spirit and the inner working of His grace which cause a person to be conformed to His image. With this as our foundation, we spent time individually and together identifying those character traits we most longed for the Lord to develop in our grandchildren. After compiling a list of traits and grouping them into twelve categories—one for each month—we asked the Lord to guide and direct our prayers.

It was exciting, yet sobering, to realize that if we prayed "effective and fervent prayers" on behalf of our grandchildren, our sovereign and good God promises to hear those prayers and answer them. As the Lord gave form to our prayers, He also impressed upon us the importance of reinforcing the development of the character traits through applications. Thus, on each day's entry, we have included a verse from Proverbs, a prayer specific to that verse, and an activity that allows grandmother and grandchild to interact in a practical application of the truth.

We know there are limitations to the prayers and activities as written. For example, we found that it proved too awkward to write each prayer for both grandsons and granddaughters, and so we alternated. One day, our prayers utilize the feminine pronouns for our grandchildren and the next day, the male pronouns. The prayers, however, are designed for both boys and girls. We encourage the reader to pray the prayer on behalf of a grandchild, perhaps inserting the name.

We also realize that in our variety of applications, some may be more appropriate for younger children and others for those who are older. Each application is meant to jumpstart the reader's own creativity. We acknowledge and delight in the diversity of our readers, and encourage them to adapt the application section to their unique needs, locations, and resources.

In categorizing the character traits, we recognized that often there was overlap of two or three characteristics contained in a single verse. The reader may think that a verse categorized under the trait "Graciousness" might be more appropriate under "Wisdom." We wrestled with this dilemma, prayed through the verses, and made the best decisions we could. We are well aware, however, that others might have chosen differently.

We are three very ordinary women, three grandmothers who believe in the faithfulness of God. Our hearts' desire is simply and profoundly to implore the Lord to equip the next generations to stand strong in their faith. While we want our grandchildren to know that we are praying for them—regularly, specifically, fervently—we are even more concerned that they know our God and His promise to hear and answer those who call on Him. It is our earnest prayer that, early in life, our grandchildren will come to accept Jesus Christ as their personal Savior and Lord, which will equip them to be godly men and women, able to influence the world with the gospel.

For you, dear reader, we pray a sense of God's presence and leading as these prayers are uttered on behalf of this next generation. We pray that your own faith will be strengthened and that you will experience God's blessings. Finally, we pray that God would enable us all to leave a legacy of faith so that He might be honored and glorified. May we proclaim together Psalm 89:1-2: "I will sing of the Lord's great love forever; with my mouth I will make your faithfulness known through all generations. I will declare that your love stands firm forever, that you established your faithfulness in heaven itself."

As you read these Scriptures and pray these prayers, we want you to know that we are praying for *you*.

MAY MY GRANDCHILD DEMONSTRATE...

FAITHFULNESS

JANUARY

January 1

"Like the cold of snow in time of harvest
is a faithful messenger to those
who send him, for he refreshes
the soul of his masters."

– Proverbs 25:13 (NKJV)

Lord, I pray that my grandchild's faithfulness
will be an encouragement to everyone she meets.
May she know that You are pleased when she seeks You
and that her faith can be a refreshment to others.
May she be known as a steadfast messenger
of Your Word and a dependable friend to all.

Application: Enjoy a cup of hot chocolate with your grandchild on a cold winter's day. Discuss how God's Word tells us that our faith can be just like a refreshing treat when we share it with others.

January 2

"Trust in the LORD with all your heart and lean not on your own understanding; in all your ways acknowledge him, and he will make your paths straight."

—PROVERBS 3:5-6

Father, it is tempting for Your children to take detours that lead them astray. But I pray that my grandchild will trust You to keep his feet on a straight path. Thank You for giving him this Bible promise—that as he acknowledges You in everything he does, You will guide him to safety.

Application: Take a walk in your neighborhood and discuss the best path to take to arrive at your destination. Reassure your grandchild that no matter what difficulties he may face in life, God will be there to walk with him.

January 3

"He who fears the LORD has a secure fortress, and for his children it will be a refuge."

—PROVERBS 14: 26

Lord, You are our refuge, and we thank You for Your protection. May my grandchild embrace You in faith at an early age and learn to trust You. Help her to understand that Your promises are like a strong fortress, providing safety and security for Your children in an ever-changing world.

<u>Application:</u> Build a fortress together out of materials you may have at home—Legos, building blocks, popsicle sticks, etc.—and discuss how a fortress provides protection.

January 4

"Like a bad tooth or a lame foot
is reliance on the unfaithful
in times of trouble."

—PROVERBS 25:19

Lord, I pray that my grandchild will learn that, even though his friends may let him down, You are the ultimate example of faithfulness in times of trouble. I pray that You will also send him faithful friends who would lead him to a deeper walk with You. Help him to be trustworthy, one who can be counted among the faithful when troubles arise.

Application: Play a game of hopscotch with your grandchild. Talk about how hard it would be to play this game if he had a sore foot and how much more stable he is when he uses both feet. Discuss the importance of stability and reliability in times of trouble.

January 5

"The fear of the LORD
is the beginning of wisdom,
and knowledge of the Holy One
is understanding."

—PROVERBS 9:10

Lord, please help my grandchild to understand fear of You—a balance of awe and reverence with approachability. Help her to respect You as the Creator and Sustainer of the universe and the ultimate Judge of all mankind. Yet at the same time, let her know that she can call, "Abba-Papa!" and You will answer. Help her, Lord, to be faithful in her pursuit of You.

Application: Read Psalm 100 with your grandchild so that you can rejoice in the Lord. For an extra challenge, memorize this psalm together.

January 6

"A wicked messenger falls into trouble,
but a trustworthy envoy brings healing."

—PROVERBS 13:17

Lord, I pray that You would allow my grandchild to faithfully deliver Your words of encouragement to those around him. Help him to see how speaking truth can heal a heavy heart and mind. It is sobering to realize that not speaking truth can lead us into trouble, and I pray that my grandchild will not have to experience that reality.

Application: Talk about the many ways we can bring healing to others—counseling, friendship, encouraging words—and how speaking the truth in love is always the best way to communicate.

January 7

"For he guards the course of the just
and protects the way of his faithful ones.
Then you will understand what is right
and just and fair—every good path."

—Proverbs 2:8-9

Lord, I thank You that You are our Guardian. I pray that my grandchild would faithfully trust Your guardianship in every area of her life. Help her to know that You are also her Protector. May she desire at an early age to follow the path You lay out for her and to understand what is right, just, and fair.

Application: Memorize with your grandchild Romans 16:19b: "I want you to be wise in what is good and innocent in what is evil."

January 8

"He who earnestly seeks good finds favor,
but trouble will come to him
who seeks evil."

—Proverbs 11:27 (NKJV)

*Father, You alone are entirely good.
Please help my grandchild to be faithful in seeking Your goodness. Help him focus his heart on the loveliness found in Jesus. May he be grounded in Your Word so that Your Spirit can conform his character to that of Christ.
Please bless him with Your favor as he strives to honor You in all that he does.*

Application: Play Hide and Seek with your grandchild and discuss how this verse tells us to seek God and His goodness, and we will find favor.

January 9

"The fear of the LORD teaches a man wisdom, and humility comes before honor."

—PROVERBS 15:33

Lord, I pray that my grandchild will gain wisdom through a healthy fear of Your majesty and sovereignty. Allow her to see You as You are so that she will be more likely to see herself as she is—unworthy of Your love and in need of Your grace. Give her a spirit of humility that allows her faith to grow so that she can please You.

<u>Application:</u> Teach your grandchild about humility by following Jesus' example of washing feet. Have her sit in a chair and remove her shoes and socks. Then wash her feet, demonstrating the tenderness and love of Jesus.

January 10

"The path of life leads upward for the wise, to keep him from going down to the grave."

—PROVERBS 15:24

Father, Your Word tells us that just as the heavens are higher than the earth, Your ways and thoughts are higher than ours (see Isaiah 55:9). I pray that Your Holy Spirit would cause my grandchild's mind and affections to dwell upon Jesus, the One who sits in heaven at Your right hand. Give him the power to be faithful in pursuing a life here on earth that is controlled by a heavenly focus.

Application: Take a look at the sky on a starry night and discuss with your grandchild how God's ways and thoughts are higher than ours and that His majesty is proclaimed through His creation.

January 11

"A greedy man stirs up dissension,
but he who trusts in the LORD will prosper."

—PROVERBS 28:25

Lord, I thank You that You prosper people in many different ways. If material prosperity is one of the ways You choose to bless my grandchild, I pray that she will be known for her generosity, not for greed. As she trusts You to provide for her, spiritually as well as materially, I pray that she will always have more than enough of everything to share with others—and then be faithful to share it.

Application: Play games with your grandchild that require her to "trust" you—jumping into your arms, holding her hand as she balances on a bar, blindfolding her while taking a walk together, etc. Discuss how we sometimes need to trust the Lord even when we don't know where He is leading us.

January 12

"The fear of the Lord
is the beginning of knowledge,
but fools despise wisdom and discipline."

– Proverbs 1:7

O Father, help my grandchild to honor You as God Almighty—Creator and Sovereign Lord of all the earth. Help him to understand that You are all-powerful and to revere You above all else. Please allow him to be faithful in his walk with You and to desire Your wisdom and discipline because they lead to greater knowledge of You.

Application: Talk to your grandchild about the Bible's admonition to fear the Lord. Discuss how "fear of the Lord" is similar to reverence of the Lord—a realization of His power, might, and goodness—and that it does not mean to be afraid of Him.

January 13

"A wise man attacks the city of the mighty
and pulls down the stronghold
in which they trust."

—Proverbs 21:22

Father, this verse contradicts our world's view that "might makes right." Please teach my grandchild not to trust in her own strength. Instead, enable her to place her confidence in You, the only stronghold that will endure. Fill her heart and mind with the words of the psalmist, "I love You, O Lord, my strength" (Psalm 18:1).

<u>Application:</u> Read the story of David and Goliath (see 1 Samuel 17:1-51). Point out how God blessed David when he trusted in Him rather than in worldly weapons, physical strength, or skill.

January 14

"The faithless will be fully repaid for their ways, and the good man rewarded for his."

—Proverbs 14:14

Lord, I pray that my grandchild would reap the rewards of a faithful life. Help him to live in a manner that is so full of trust in You that he is filled with love, joy, and peace. Allow him to be bold in pursuing works for Your kingdom and to believe that You will complete all things according to Your will. Help his faith to be a light and an example to others.

<u>Application:</u> Learn about Corrie ten Boom by either reading her book, *The Hiding Place*, or watching the movie of the same name. You may also find information on the Internet. Discuss how Corrie's faith directed everything she did.

January 15

"Fear of man will prove to be a snare,
but whoever trusts in the LORD is kept safe."

—Proverbs 29:25

Lord, I pray that You would help my grandchild to trust You in all circumstances of life. May she always be secure in Your care. Help her to understand that she must live her life, not according to the expectations of man, but according to Your desires. Bless her so that as her faith in You grows, her fear of man—attempting to please people more than You—will diminish.

Application: Read Daniel 1:8-18 to your grandchild and discuss the story of Daniel and his choice to obey God rather than man. Point out that God kept Daniel safe in difficult and challenging circumstances.

January 16

"A longing fulfilled is sweet to the soul,
but fools detest turning from evil."

—Proverbs 13:19

Father, I ask that my grandchild would long for You and Your Word. Please give him a faithful spirit that pursues good and not evil. Make him aware of the temptations of this world and help him to stay clear of activities that would lead him away from You. Even if foolish friends try to persuade him to join them in their sin, may his faith in You give him the strength to resist.

Application: Tell your grandchild about a gift you longed for as a child and how you felt when you received it. Remind him that God loves to give His children sweet surprises, too, especially to those who remain faithful to Him!

January 17

"A wise man has great power,
and a man of knowledge increases strength."

—Proverbs 24:5

Lord, there is no one as powerful as You; however, this verse tells us that as people gain knowledge and wisdom, they also gain power. I pray that my grandchild will come to understand that while worldly knowledge leads to a certain kind of "success," it is faith and godly wisdom that bring strength of character and please You.

Application: Teach your grandchild how to arm wrestle. Discuss the different kinds of strength she can gain with a faithful exercise regimen—physical, mental, spiritual. Talk about what it will take to build *spiritual* muscle.

January 18

"A king delights in a wise servant,
but a shameful servant incurs his wrath."

—Proverbs 14:35

O Lord, my King, thank You for Your faithfulness and devotion to Your people. I pray that You would enable my grandchild to be a wise and loyal servant in Your kingdom. Please help his faithfulness to You overflow into every area of his life. Help him to sense Your delight as he makes wise and prudent choices.

Application: Discuss with your grandchild what happens when people make wise decisions in their jobs: Doctors provide excellent care, police officers keep others safe, teachers impart knowledge, etc.

January 19

"Do not be wise in your own eyes;
fear the LORD and shun evil.
This will bring health to your body and
nourishment to your bones."

—PROVERBS 3:7-8

Lord, please help my grandchild to have such respect and fear of You that she will literally run away from evil! Develop in her a strong and vibrant faith that desires Your wisdom and goodness. Please give her the physical and spiritual health that comes from a right understanding of who You are.

Application: Enjoy a healthy snack together. Discuss how your grandchild's faith, like this healthy snack, is food for her spirit.

January 20

"Have no fear of sudden disaster or
of the ruin that overtakes the wicked,
for the LORD will be your confidence
and will keep your foot from being snared."

—PROVERBS 3:25-26

Lord, please remind my grandchild that You are faithful in both good times and bad. He need never be afraid of "sudden disasters" because Your promises are trustworthy. Lord, I thank You that even though there is evil in the world, You will protect him and keep him from falling into one of the enemy's traps. Strengthen his faith in You, the God who keeps His promises.

Application: Talk about what happens when a small animal—a mouse, a rabbit, or a raccoon—is caught in a trap. The little animal may suffer and is definitely stuck and cannot experience freedom. Even though we may sometimes feel "trapped," God knows how to care for us and will be with us always.

January 21

"The prudent see danger and take refuge, but the simple keep going and suffer for it."

Proverbs 27:12

Lord, I pray that You will give my grandchild the ability to recognize the many faces of evil in this dangerous and deceptive world. Please strengthen her faith so that she may not be so foolish as to ignore the danger signals and have to suffer the consequences. Help her to run to You when she is threatened and to take comfort in You as her refuge.

Application: Discuss how Jesus used the Word of God in dealing with temptation in the wilderness (see Matthew 4:1-11).

January 22

"Do not let your heart envy sinners,
but always be zealous
for the fear of the LORD.
There is surely a future hope for you,
and your hope will not be cut off."

—PROVERBS 23:17-18

Father, we acknowledge You as the God of all hope and comfort. I pray that my grandchild will never envy or want to be involved with those who break Your laws. Help him, instead, to zealously pursue You and to know that his greatest hope for the future is Jesus and that he will always be safe with Him.

Application: Memorize Jeremiah 29:11 with your grandchild: "'For I know the plans I have for you,' declares the LORD, 'plans to prosper you and not to harm you, plans to give you hope and a future.'"

January 23

"The horse is made ready
for the day of battle,
but victory rests with the LORD."

—PROVERBS 21:31

Lord, we are grateful for Your faithfulness each day of our lives. Thank You for reminding us that though we are to prepare for difficult days ahead, You know what each day will bring. I pray that You will strengthen my grandchild's faith by helping her to walk closely with You. Help her, too, to experience Your victories during the battles of her life.

Application: Take your grandchild to the park or to a shopping mall and let her ride on a carousel horse. Discuss how horses were trained for battle in Bible times. Then talk about how we can prepare for difficulties in our own life by seeking to know God and His Word.

January 24

"He who pursues righteousness
and love finds life,
prosperity and honor."

—Proverbs 21:21

Lord, thank You for Your faithful love to my grandchild. Please help him to respond to that love and to know that You are the Love and Righteousness he needs to pursue. Give him the faith to move forward in seeking You. Bless him with an abundant life, one full of joy and honor, as he comes to know You better.

Application: Share with your grandchild that one way some people receive special recognition and honor is to be given a crown. The Bible says that if we love the Lord, we will receive a crown of righteousness (see 2 Timothy 4:7-8). Together make a crown out of construction paper, decorate it, and write on it the word *Righteous.*

January 25

"Good understanding wins favor,
but the way of the unfaithful is hard."

—Proverbs 13:15

Father, thank You for all the wise warnings in Your Word. Please help my grandchild to take Your advice to heart and to be Your faithful follower. Help her to recognize any rebellion in herself so she can turn from it and the "hard" consequences it may bring. I pray that, like Jesus, she will grow "in wisdom and stature, and in favor with God and men" (Luke 2:52).

Application: Discuss with your grandchild how she can "grow in wisdom, stature, and in favor with God and men." Suggest such activities as reading the Bible, eating healthy foods, and choosing godly friends.

January 26

"Better a little with the fear of the LORD than great wealth with turmoil."

--PROVERBS 15:16

Lord, help my grandchild to have faith that is demonstrated through reverent fear and trust in You. Help him to be thankful for all that You provide, whether it be little or much. I pray that his life would be a reflection of gratitude for Your blessings. Help him to be confident that You will always meet his needs.

Application: Make a blessing box with your grandchild. Fill it with notes of things for which you are thankful. Read one blessing together each day.

January 27

"Pay attention and listen to the sayings of the wise; apply your heart to what I teach, for it is pleasing when you keep them in your heart and have all of them ready on your lips. So that your trust may be in the LORD, I teach you today, even you."

– PROVERBS 22:17-19

Lord, please make my grandchild receptive to learning Your Word ....today! May she come to love the "dailyness" of trusting You and knowing that Your mercies are new every morning. Please help her faithfully establish a regular time to read Your Word and listen to Your voice for instruction. May she store these nuggets of wisdom in her heart, then "have all of them ready on (her) lips" to share with others.

Application: Talk about daily habits—brushing teeth, combing hair, eating, etc.—and how necessary they are for life. Share with your grandchild that the daily habits of faith—reading God's Word and prayer—are even more important…and will last forever!

January 28

"A gossip betrays a confidence,
but a trustworthy man keeps a secret."

—Proverbs 11:13

Lord, I pray that my grandchild will learn early the destructiveness of gossip. Please give him the desire to be a faithful friend who listens well and can keep a confidence. Help him to discern when to be silent and when to speak. Thank You that he can then be known as a trustworthy friend.

<u>Application:</u> Read the story of Samson and Delilah (see Judges 16:1-20) and discuss how Delilah betrayed Samson by sharing his secret.

January 29

"Through love and faithfulness
sin is atoned for; through the fear of the LORD
a man avoids evil."

—PROVERBS 16:6

Lord God, You gave my grandchild the ultimate gift of love—Your Son—who died on the cross for her sins. Please help her to understand, while she is still young, that she is a sinner who needs the Savior. Then help her follow the example of Jesus, who lived His life in faithfulness and obedience to His Father. May she love and honor You so much that evil has no appeal for her.

Application: Make a salvation book. Take one sheet each of black, red, white, green, and gold construction paper. Cut the papers into a desired size and staple them together in the order listed above. Then share the story with a friend: "We were **black** with sin. Christ's rich, **red** blood was shed for those sins. Through faith, we become **white** as snow and as we grow in Him, we experience new life **(green).** Finally, we will walk forever in heaven with Him on streets of **gold."**

January 30

"Every word of God is flawless, he is a shield to those who take refuge in him."

—Proverbs 30:5

Father, we are grateful that Your Holy Scriptures are perfect. You have given them to my grandchild to show him how to live. Please give him a love for Your Word and a desire to live a life governed by Your principles. As he hides Your Word in his heart, help him to feel completely protected and shielded from all eternal harm.

Application: Give your grandchild a Bible. Be sure to include a personal inscription, reassuring him of your love and God's love for him.

January 31

"A faithful man will be richly blessed,
but one eager to get rich
will not go unpunished."

—Proverbs 28:20

Lord, I pray that You would help my grandchild to learn patience in all aspects of life—faith, relationships, finances, education, health, and development of character. Help her to trust You to bring forth Your design in her life and to embrace the process of growth. May Your blessings flow and her faith grow as she practices faithfulness.

Application: Tell your grandchild the story of "The Tortoise and the Hare." Emphasize the fact that slow and steady progress—another way to look at *faithfulness*—wins the race.

MAY MY GRANDCHILD BE...

TEACHABLE

FEBRUARY

February 1

"The purpose of Proverbs:
to know wisdom and instruction,
to perceive the words of understanding,
to receive the instruction of wisdom, justice,
judgment and equity."

—Proverbs 1: 2-3 (NKJV)

Lord, thank You for this wonderfully wise and practical book called Proverbs. Please give my grandchild a teachable heart that is open to the fatherly instruction found here. May he love these words and desire to apply them to his life. Help him to know that it is only Your wisdom that results in true justice and righteousness.

Application: Make a small book of several favorite proverbs. Let your grandchild illustrate the pages and then talk about how these proverbs apply to his life.

February 2

"Listen to your father, who gave you life,
and do not despise your mother
when she is old."

—PROVERBS 23:22

*Lord, I thank You for my grandchild's parents.
I pray that she will learn to appreciate her father and mother and that, early in life, she will value relationships with other family members across the generations.
Help her to respect her father and listen to his advice, and to show love and understanding for her mother.*

Application: Choose an activity with your grandchild that will demonstrate love and respect for her parents. Some suggestions might be: Pick some flowers, draw a picture, serve breakfast in bed, make a favorite dessert…

February 3

"Blessed is the man who finds wisdom,
the man who gains understanding."

—Proverbs 3:13

Lord, please develop in my grandchild a teachable spirit—one that thirsts for wisdom. Help him to experience the blessings that result from acquiring understanding. I ask, however, that he would never be satisfied with what he knows, only whom he knows. May his ultimate goal be to know You, the One who imparts all wisdom.

Application: Play a game of "Trivial Pursuit" with your grandchild. Discuss how many fun facts you need to know in order to play this game successfully. While these are important to the game, the most important truths for living a successful life are found in the Bible.

February 4

"Choose my instruction instead of silver, knowledge rather than choice gold."

– Proverbs 8:10

Lord, thank You for reminding us that instruction from You is better than all the wealth of the world. I pray that my grandchild will love You and Your ways more than riches and material possessions. Please give her insight as to the fleeting nature of gold and silver, compared to the permanence of Your Word. Help her to have a teachable spirit so that she may wholeheartedly delight in the wondrous lessons You teach her.

Application: Blow bubbles with your grandchild and talk about how they are like riches—beautiful for the moment, but soon passing away. Remind your grandchild that only God's Word and His truth are everlasting.

February 5

"A word aptly spoken is like apples of gold in settings of silver."

—Proverbs 25:11

Lord, the word picture of "apples of gold in settings of silver" conveys wealth, richness, and desirability. I pray that my grandchild's words would have the same characteristics. Please help him to learn about You so that his words reveal a wealth of character, a rich understanding of Scripture, and a desire to minister to others.

Application: Paint or color a picture of golden apples in a silver bowl. Share this proverb with your grandchild and discuss its meaning—that tactful, timely, and appropriate words can impart understanding and encouragement.

February 6

"Plans fail for lack of counsel,
but with many advisers they succeed."

—Proverbs 15:22

Lord, some situations call for the accumulated wisdom of godly men and women. I pray that my grandchild would know how and when to seek the advice of others. Please assure her that this does not reveal personal weakness, but rather demonstrates maturity and wisdom. Please instill in her a humble heart, ready and willing to listen to wise counsel.

Application: Paraphrase the story of Esther and Mordecai from the Book of Esther in the Bible. Make puppets out of paper bags—one for Esther and one for Mordecai—and act out the story. Emphasize how Esther continually sought the wise counsel of her uncle, Mordecai, who represents the role of the Holy Spirit as her Teacher and Counselor.

February 7

"Listen, my son, to your father's instruction and do not forsake your mother's teaching."

—Proverbs 1:8

Father, I pray that the instruction from my grandchild's parents would always be wise and gracious. I ask that You would help them be consistent models in their words and actions. Please help my grandchild to be willing to listen, learn, and live out their instruction.

Application: Find a favorite recipe and make a special treat together. Then discuss the benefits of following instructions.

February 8

"My son, pay attention to what I say;
listen closely to my words."

—Proverbs 4:20

Father, please give my grandchild the ability to focus on You and Your Word in a world where so many distractions are vying for her attention. Help her to understand the importance of being teachable and giving close attention to Your instruction. May she be known as someone who not only hears the Word, but applies and practices it as well.

Application: Sing the "B-I-B-L-E Song." It goes like this: "The B-I-B-L-E, yes that's the book for me. I'll stand alone on the Word of God, the B-I-B-L-E. BIBLE!"

February 9

"Let your eyes look straight ahead,
fix your gaze directly before you.
Make level paths for your feet
and take only ways that are firm.
Do not swerve to the right or the left;
keep your foot from evil."

– Proverbs 4:25-27

Lord, thank You for the detailed directives You give us in these verses. Please give my grandchild the desire to know and follow each one! May he not be attracted by the temptations of this life, but instead keep his eyes on the path You set before him so that he will not stumble into the traps set by the world.

<u>Application:</u> Play the Hokey Pokey game with your grandchild. Sing together: "Put your right foot in, take your right foot out; put your left foot in, take your left foot out..." Explain that this game helps us understand God's plan to keep us safe by not "swerving" to the right or left, but staying on His straight path.

February 10

"My son, keep my words and store up my commands within you. Keep my commands and you will live; guard my teachings as the apple of your eye. Bind them on your fingers; write them on the tablet of your heart. Say to wisdom, 'You are my sister,' and call understanding your kinsman."

--Proverbs 7:1-4

Lord, this verse tells us that Your words are like treasured members of our family. I pray that my grandchild would cherish Your words in her heart and never forsake their teaching. Help her to understand that not only do Your commandments teach us how *to live…they* are *life! May she guard them like precious jewels and never forget them.*

Application: Tie a string around your grandchild's finger. Tell her that when she looks at it, she can remember that God's Word tells her how much He loves her.

February 11

"He who answers before listening—that is his folly and his shame."

—Proverbs 18:13

Lord, the Book of James reminds us that we should all be "quick to listen, slow to speak, and slow to become angry" (1:19). Please help my grandchild take these words to heart. Help him to listen carefully to others in order to better understand what they are saying, and respond wisely. Please let him be known as an astute and thoughtful communicator, not as one who jumps to hasty conclusions and speaks without thinking.

Application: Ask your grandchild to share with you three fun things that happened to him during the day. Demonstrate good listening skills by asking specific questions about those stories and responding appropriately.

February 12

"He who ignores discipline despises himself,
but whoever heeds correction
gains understanding."

—Proverbs 15:32

Lord, we know that sometimes the best learning comes through discipline. I pray that my grandchild will be receptive to receiving correction from others. Help her to understand this paradox: Ignoring the hard lessons that will build character and help her grow actually means that she despises herself— "looks down on herself with contempt."

Application: Make a stop sign out of construction paper and tape it onto a stick. Using the homemade sign, play a game of "Stop and Go" with your grandchild. Reinforce the fact that rules should be followed for our own protection and safety.

February 13

"Listen to advice and accept instruction,
and in the end you will be wise."

—Proverbs 19:20

Lord, this counsel from Your Word seems so simple, yet it is so challenging. I pray that my grandchild would be a discerning listener and accept good advice and instruction when it is offered. Help him to see that the end result of such action will be wisdom. And, please, Lord, allow him to know You as the Source of all wisdom.

Application: Attend church with your grandchild. After the service, share what you have both learned.

February 14

"Stop listening to instruction,
my son, and you will stray
from the words of knowledge."

— Proverbs 19:27

Lord, many verses in the Book of Proverbs admonish us to listen and be wise. This verse is a warning about what will happen if my grandchild stops listening to godly instruction: She may stray from Your Word and miss Your best plans for her life! I pray, Lord, that my grandchild will be committed to a lifetime of learning about You and would not wander from that path.

Application: Encourage your grandchild to read Scripture. Make a chart to show her progress. Celebrate with a special treat when she finishes a book of the Bible.

February 15

"Train a child in the way he should go,
and when he is old he will not turn from it."

—PROVERBS 22:6

Lord, I thank You that children, like clay, are capable of being molded. I pray that my grandchild's parents will take their job seriously and that we, as grandparents, will give them the support they need. And, Lord, please give my grandchild a heart that welcomes instruction and will never turn from it all of his life!

Application: Make a habit of praying with your grandchild before each meal you eat together. Take turns thanking God for the food, giving your grandchild practical experience and making memories that will last a lifetime.

February 16

"Hold on to instruction, do not let it go; guard it well, for it is your life."

—Proverbs 4:13

Lord, please give my grandchild the tenacity to hold onto Your instruction. Help her to embrace Scripture truths; allow her heart and mind to be open to learning what Your Word reveals. Thank You that all of Scripture points to Jesus, the very Source of all life. Bless her with a relationship with You and the assurance of eternal life.

Application: Take your grandchild to the circus or find a book or movie about a circus. Tell her to watch the trapeze artists as they hold onto the bar and speculate what might happen if they let go. Unless there is a net underneath to break their fall, they might be seriously injured or even lose their lives! Likewise, for our own safety, we need to hold onto God's instruction.

February 17

"He who listens to a life-giving rebuke will be at home among the wise."

—Proverbs 15:31

Father, it is never easy to hear someone criticize what we are doing, so I pray that my grandchild would receive thoughtful criticism as a challenge to do what is right. Give him a teachable spirit as he listens and learns from those who are older and wiser. May those who criticize do so with grace and love.

Application: Teach your grandchild the fire safety rule: "Stop, drop and roll!" Explain that this is one type of instruction that will not only make him wise, but will save his life!

February 18

"Do not rebuke a mocker or he will hate you; rebuke a wise man and he will love you. Instruct a wise man and he will be wiser still; teach a righteous man and he will add to his learning."

—Proverbs 9:8-9

Lord, thank You for the acknowledgment that people who are wise appreciate instruction and correction. Give my grandchild the desire to learn; help her to receive instruction in righteousness as a gift from You. Help her to have a humble spirit, willing to admit her mistakes and eager to learn from those who are sent by You with godly correction.

Application: Read James 1:5 together: "If anyone lacks wisdom, he should ask God, who gives generously to all without finding fault, and it will be given to him." Pray together for God's wisdom and for faithfulness in applying it.

February 19

"He who scorns instruction will pay for it, but he who respects a command is rewarded."

—Proverbs 13:13

Lord, we are reminded in this verse that there are consequences for our actions. If we ignore instruction, we will face difficulty; if we respect instruction, there will be a reward. I pray that You would give my grandchild a heart to receive Your teaching. Please help him to honor Your Word and the counsel of godly men and women.

Application: Take your grandchild to visit a pet store or an animal shelter. Ask the caretakers to tell you how they train their animals. How are the animals treated when they obey a command? They are rewarded, aren't they? Similarly, this proverb says that we are rewarded when we respect God's commands.

February 20

"My son, do not forget my teaching,
but keep my commands in your heart."

—Proverbs 3:1

Father, thank You for giving Your people commandments by which to live. May my grandchild delight in reading and studying all You have spoken. Please also help her to understand the importance of storing Your Word in her heart. Make her life a shining example of one who knows You and walks closely with You.

Application: Play a "matching" card game with your grandchild. Place the cards face down and try to choose cards that match. The person with the most matches wins. Discuss how important it is to store information in our memory—especially the life-giving Word of God.

February 21

"But whoever listens to me will live in safety and be at ease, without fear of harm."

—PROVERBS 1:33

Lord, thank You for giving us the assurance that if we listen to You, we will be safe in Your keeping. Please help my grandchild to learn about Your great love for him. May he be confident that "perfect love drives out fear" (1 John 4:18). Please build in him the security of knowing that You are always with him, in every place, and at all times.

Application: Together memorize God's promise in Genesis 28:15a: "I am with you and will watch over you wherever you go."

February 22

"He who rebukes a man
will in the end gain more favor
than he who has a flattering tongue."

--Proverbs 28:23

Lord, I thank You that true friends can be trusted to correct as well as to affirm. I am also grateful that Your Word instructs us to be honest in our conversation and not to flatter others to get what we want. I pray that You would teach my grandchild how to be a good friend. Help her not to hide from the truth just because it may be difficult, but to speak the truth at all times.

Application: Find an old T-shirt and some permanent markers or paint. With your grandchild, make a list of words that describe friendship and then help her paint those words on the T-shirt as a permanent reminder of the characteristics of true friends.

February 23

"He who heeds discipline
shows the way to life,
but whoever ignores correction
leads others astray."

-- Proverbs 10:17

Father, it is humbling to realize that our actions can have such a significant impact on others. This verse declares that our rebellion can not only get us into trouble, but can also lead others astray. I pray that my grandchild will have a heart that is receptive to Your ways. Help him to understand that every single choice he makes has consequences—for either good or bad. I ask, Lord, that he will make choices that would lead others to You.

Application: Stage a treasure hunt with your grandchild. Hide a small gift ahead of time, then place clues around your home leading to the prize. Explain that the way we live our lives can also point others to the ultimate prize of knowing the Lord.

February 24

"Let the wise listen and add to their learning, and let the discerning get guidance."

—Proverbs 1:5

Thank You, Lord, for teaching us that You are the Source of all true wisdom. Please help my grandchild be a teachable student of Your Word. May she be able to discern the difference between biblical and worldly wisdom, always seeking guidance from godly counselors. Give her the desire to apply Your Word to every decision of her life.

Application: Read the story of Josiah, the young boy who became king of Israel at the age of eight (see 2 Kings 22:1-2). Discuss how King Josiah had to learn quickly and demonstrate wisdom at a very early age.

February 25

"My son, keep your father's commands and do not forsake your mother's teaching... For these commands are a lamp, this teaching is a light,and the corrections of discipline are the way to life."

--Proverbs 6:20, 23

Father, please help my grandchild to view guidance from his parents as a light to help him "see" how to make good decisions. Please keep him from rebelling against their teaching; instead, allow him to understand that these instructions lead to life at its best. I ask that he not settle for immediate gratification and ignore the long-term benefits of discipline. And, please, Lord, shine Your own light on his path so he knows how to follow You.

Application: Prepare a simple, fun meal with your grandchild and eat it by candlelight. Point out how even a small candle makes a big difference in the dark.

February 26

"If anyone turns a deaf ear to the law, even his prayers are detestable."

—Proverbs 28:9

Lord, I thank You for Your guidelines for our lives and for instructing us that Your Old Testament laws were established to keep Your people safe, healthy, and blessed. I am also eternally grateful that Jesus fulfilled the requirements of the law by His death on the cross. I pray that my grandchild will have a teachable and open heart to receive Your greatest gift, Jesus. May she come to know Him, understand her need to repent of her sins, and accept forgiveness so that her prayers may be pleasing to You.

Application: Encourage your grandchild to keep a prayer journal. Show her how to list the prayer prayed and then to anticipate a time when God will answer that prayer. Tell her to be sure to record the date!

February 27

"When a wise man is instructed,
he gets knowledge.'

—Proverbs 21:11b

Lord, thank You for the simple truth that when instruction is given, it can either be accepted or rejected. I pray that my grandchild will choose to thoughtfully receive godly counsel and guidance and will not refuse it. Help him to grow in knowledge, wisdom, and understanding—especially in His knowledge of Your Word and Your ways.

<u>Application:</u> Choose an activity that demonstrates a specific teaching in God's Word—for example, giving. Teach your grandchild about the important spiritual discipline of tithing (giving to the Lord a tenth of your resources, including time). Together give a gift of your time by volunteering in a Sunday school class or helping a family in need.

February 28

"The wise in heart accept commands,
but a chattering fool comes to ruin."

—Proverbs 10:8

Father, how difficult it is to be quiet in a busy, noisy world! Please help my grandchild learn to appreciate the advantages of being still. Make her receptive to the words in Scripture which will make her wise. Develop in her a thoughtful and obedient heart and lead her in the paths of wisdom and righteousness for Your name's sake.

Application: Challenge your grandchild to be quiet for a little while. Ask her to remember what she heard and observed during that quiet time. Point out how having a still spirit and a listening heart will help her to notice things she might ordinarily miss.

February 29

"Whoever gives heed to instruction
prospers, and blessed is he
who trusts in the LORD."

—PROVERBS 16:20

Lord, please give my grandchild an attentive ear to those who are teaching him. Whether it be at home, at school, or at church, give him a desire to learn—especially truths about You. Thank You for the blessings that will follow if he seeks to know and trust You. Even when he is uncertain about the best choices to make, help him to believe that You know what is best and will guide him to a good destination.

Application: Demonstrate the concept of trust by blindfolding your grandchild and leading him into a different room. Explain that this is similar to our need to trust God as He leads us. Say, "If you can trust me to guide you, think how much more you can trust your heavenly Father, who made you and who has promised never to leave you."

MAY MY GRANDCHILD LEARN...

DISCIPLINE

MARCH

March 1

"The wise shall inherit glory,
but shame shall be the legacy of fools."

—Proverbs 3:35 (NKJV)

Father, we acknowledge that all the treasures of perfect wisdom are found in Jesus. I pray for my grandchild to become steadfast and disciplined in her pursuit of Him from her earliest years. As she grows in her faith, please give her more and more of Your wisdom. May she also learn to appreciate the glory of the inheritance and the richness of eternal life that is hers because of what Jesus has done for her.

Application: Discuss with your grandchild what you would like to leave her as your spiritual legacy or inheritance. Ask if she has any thoughts about what she would like to leave *her* children as her spiritual legacy one day.

March 2

"Lazy hands make a man poor,
but diligent hands bring wealth."

—Proverbs 10:4

Lord, we acknowledge that neither You nor the world owes us anything in this life. In Your great mercy, Father, You have created work for us to do and have given us relationships to nurture. Help my grandchild learn to be diligent in all aspects of his life. Please enable him to experience all the benefits—the "wealth"—that discipline brings when he is faithful in his profession, in his ministry, and in his relationships with others.

Application: Help your grandchild write a note or card to someone special, thanking that person for his or her hard work and diligence.

March 3

"Listen, my son, and be wise, and keep your heart on the right path. Do not join those who drink too much wine or gorge themselves on meat, for drunkards and gluttons become poor, and drowsiness clothes them in rags."

—Proverbs 23:19-21

Lord, You have blessed us with so much in the way of physical provisions. Please help my grandchild to be thankful for all You have provided. Let her guard her heart and exhibit self-control so that Your blessings will not be abused. Father, give her the wisdom to stay away from those who inappropriately use Your gifts. May the discipline in her life be a beacon of hope and encouragement to others who are watching.

Application: Discuss with your grandchild the importance of a healthy lifestyle. Explain the choices she needs to make to stay healthy. Help her understand that what may be appropriate in small amounts will not be appropriate in excess—food, drink, etc.

March 4

"As a door turns on its hinges,
so does the lazy man on his bed."

—PROVERBS 26:14 (NKJV)

Father, Your Word tells us that "the sleep of a laborer is sweet" (Ecclesiastes 5:12). I pray for my grandchild to have sound, restful sleep that results from disciplined labor. Help him to rise early, to work hard, and to shun laziness—the temptation to "turn over" and delay the beginning of the workday. Please help him establish good habits early in life that will serve him well for the rest of his days.

Application: Discuss with your grandchild what happens when he misses a nap or does not get enough sleep at night. Not receiving the sleep we need often results in a bad attitude or poor performance in work and play. It is also true that "sleeping in"—being lazy when it's time to start the day—can have the same effect!

March 5

"Do you see a man who excels in his work?
He will stand before kings;
he will not stand before unknown men."

— Proverbs 22:29 (NKJV)

Father, our culture gives much lip service to the importance of excellence, but the actual practice seems to be more and more rare. Please help my grandchild be intentional about developing her abilities and give her the desire to excel in all that she does. Then, as she is recognized by those in authority for her work, please allow her to be bold in giving You the praise and glory.

Application: Read 1 Kings 6:1-38 with your grandchild. Point out the intricate details given for the building of the temple and how God desired excellence in its construction. Suggest that God wants to be just as involved in developing excellence in our lives and talents.

March 6

"The way of the lazy man is like a hedge of thorns, but the way of the upright is a highway."

-- Proverbs 15:19 (NKJV)

Father, we know that this proverb does not mean that "good people" will not have difficulties in life. It does mean, however, that those with certain character traits will encounter some thorny hedges—consequences based on choices they have made. Enable my grandchild to clearly see the thorns and thistles of laziness. Please help him to delight You by his diligent and hard-working spirit and to recognize that God's way is the "high" way to true happiness.

Application: Visit a nursery or florist with your grandchild to find plants with thorns or thistles. Help him to see that thorns can cause pain and explain to him that the Bible tells us that laziness, like the thorns, can make our lives difficult and painful.

March 7

"Seldom set foot in your neighbor's house—
too much of you, and he will hate you."

—Proverbs 25:17

Lord, You have wisely instructed us on how to interact with our neighbors. Please give my grandchild the wisdom and discipline to observe boundaries and to respect her neighbor's privacy, property, and time. In serving her neighbor, may my grandchild never be considered an intruder, but may she always be a welcome guest.

Application: Make a special treat with your grandchild and take it to a neighbor. Discuss, ahead of time, how long your visit should be and why it is important not to overstay your welcome.

March 8

"Go to the ant, you sluggard;
consider its ways and be wise! It has no
commander, no overseer or ruler,
yet it stores its provisions in summer,
and gathers its food at harvest."

—Proverbs 6:6-8

Lord, what an incredible life lesson we can learn by observing the ant! The order of Your universe is so vividly displayed in the actions of this little insect. Help my grandchild learn to be equally self-motivated and persistent. Instill in him a desire to work hard and prepare wisely for the future. Encourage him to commit his work and preparation to You, and please bless him as he does so.

Application: Observe an ant hill and discuss the work that ants do. Consider giving your grandchild an ant farm to watch together.

March 9

"Do not set foot on the path of the wicked
or walk in the way of evil men.
Avoid it, do not travel on it;
turn from it and go on your way."

—Proverbs 4:14-15

"Beware of the dog!" "No Trespassing!" "Stop!" Lord, some signs make it very clear what path we need to take, but others are not so apparent. I pray that my grandchild would not set one foot on the path toward wickedness. Help her to have a healthy skepticism about alluring temptations and give her the wisdom to find the direction for her life in Your Word.

Application: Teach your grandchild the children's song:

Be careful, little eyes, what you see.
Be careful, little eyes, what you see.
For the Father up above is looking down in love,
So be careful, little eyes, what you see.

March 10

"The labor of the righteous leads to life,
the wages of the wicked to sin."

—Proverbs 10:16 (NKJV)

Father, thank You for the gift of righteousness that is ours in Jesus. Thank You, also, that though our work is not perfect, it can have eternal purpose and meaning. Please help my grandchild to live a disciplined life that includes a pleasurable occupation, rewarding relationships, and a strong faith. Give him a deep desire to know Jesus and a heart that rejoices in His gift of eternal life.

Application: Discuss with your grandchild the difference between wages and gifts: Wages must be earned, but a gift, such as eternal life, is free. Together try to list all the free gifts the Lord gives us: His love, His wisdom, His peace.

March 11

"One who is slack in his work
is brother to one who destroys."

—Proverbs 18:9

Lord, we are sometimes tempted to think that laziness is not harmful. This proverb tells us differently. Please teach my grandchild that laziness is destructive to people and property alike! Enable her to be diligent so that her work would be restorative and help her see that being industrious will protect her from ruin and destruction.

Application: Discuss with your grandchild the results of not weeding the garden or maintaining the car. Explain to her that this proverb warns that negligence can cause damage to property and can even destroy relationships.

March 12

"He who loves pleasure will become poor;
whoever loves wine and oil
will never be rich."

—Proverbs 21:17

Father, as Creator, You have given us so many wonderful things to enjoy. Unfortunately, though, we sometimes indulge ourselves more than we should. I pray that my grandchild will have the wisdom to find his contentment in You and not in the pleasures of the world. Please enable him to acknowledge and enjoy these blessings, yet be aware of their power to control. Teach him the discipline he needs to keep all things in a balanced and proper perspective.

Application: Read or tell the story of the Prodigal Son in Luke 15:11-32. Discuss how the Prodigal loved pleasure so much that he spent all his money and ended up working on a farm, eating the food intended for pigs.

March 13

"Do not make friends
with a hot-tempered man,
do not associate with one easily angered,
or you may learn his ways
and get yourself ensnared."

—Proverbs 22:24-25

Father, the gift of a true friend is a very special blessing; at the same time, the wrong kind of friendship can set a trap for one's soul! I pray that my grandchild will understand the influence friends can have on her life, and will, therefore, choose her friends carefully. Surround her with those who love You and desire to walk in Your ways; may they encourage her to be disciplined in her walk with You.

Application: Discuss with your grandchild what it means to be a friend to someone and why friends are important to us. Tell her about one of your good friends and how that friendship has encouraged you to walk more closely with the Lord.

March 14

"The heart of the discerning acquires knowledge; the ears of the wise seek it out."

—Proverbs 18:15

Father, You have given us great capacity to learn. I pray that my grandchild will have the desire and discipline necessary to study and learn much about You. Give him ears to hear and a heart that seeks to practice all he receives from Your Word. Delight him with fresh discoveries of the rich treasures found only in You.

Application: Share this old adage with your grandchild: "The Lord gave us two ears and one mouth so that we can hear twice as much as we say." Discuss why it is so important to be a good listener.

March 15

"Laziness casts one into a deep sleep, and an idle person will suffer hunger."

—Proverbs 19:15 (NKJV)

Lord, You have made it quite clear that our actions have consequences. I pray that my grandchild would refuse to let laziness get a hold in her life. Please guard her mind from the subtle message of the world that a carefree life is something to be desired. Strengthen her resolve not to eat "the bread of idleness," but to pursue her activities to Your honor and glory.

Application: Do some physical exercises, like skipping or running, with your grandchild. Discuss the benefits of staying active rather than remaining idle.

March 16

"Whoever loves discipline loves knowledge, but he who hates correction is stupid."

—Proverbs 12:1

Father, You discipline those You love. Please help my grandchild understand that correction builds character and offers protection, even when it seems unpleasant. May he earnestly desire the kind of knowledge and wisdom that are essential to righteous living. Instruct him, Lord, in how to become the man You have created him to be. The writer of Proverbs tells us that anything less is just plain stupid!

Application: Ask your grandchild what he wants to be when he grows up. Discuss the importance of training and discipline in many professions. Help him think of some people who need great skill for their important jobs: mechanics, pilots, electricians, surgeons, soldiers, etc.

March 17

"All hard work brings a profit,
but mere talk leads only to poverty."

—Proverbs 14:23

Father, You have created us with the ability to communicate and we enjoy using it. Sometimes, however, we talk too much! Help my grandchild understand that hard work can be undermined by idle chatter. As she matures, let her honor You by being productive in all that she thinks, says, and does.

Application: Play the "quiet game" with your grandchild and discuss how difficult it is for us not to talk too much—or at inappropriate times.

March 18

"Do not love sleep or you will grow poor; stay awake and you will have food to spare."

—Proverbs 20:13

Lord, restful sleep is a necessary requirement for a healthy, productive life. It is when sleep becomes an idol in our lives that we get into trouble. Please help my grandchild see that there is no place for slothful living for a Christian. Give his heart and mind an eagerness to live out the gospel as he pursues his daily work. May those who know him clearly see that his zest for living comes as a natural result of his trust in You.

Application: Take your grandchild to the grocery store or bakery to buy bread. Explain that you first had to work in order to earn the money to pay for your purchase and that, without working, we may not be able to afford what we need.

March 19

"The lazy man says, 'There is a lion outside! I shall be slain in the streets!'"

—Proverbs 22:13 (NKJV)

Excuses, excuses! Lord, people have made all kinds of excuses since the beginning of time. While there is a certain amount of humor in this proverb, we know that excuses for not working can have devastating consequences. Please help my grandchild understand her duty to work hard and not to use circumstances or others to shirk her responsibility. Bless her willingness to persevere even when things are difficult or unpleasant.

Application: Take your grandchild to the zoo to see the lions and tigers. Share this verse with her and explain that some people use excuses as silly as this for failing to get their work done.

March 20

"The hand of the diligent will rule."

–Proverbs 12:24a (NKJV)

Lord, from the beginning You created men and women to work and proclaimed it "very good." Please give my grandchild a strong work ethic. Equip him with the necessary patience and perseverance to learn a skill and perform it well. Help him understand how his diligence can bring added responsibility and authority. Allow his hard work to make a positive influence on those around him and ultimately bring glory to Your name.

Application: Work with your grandchild on a project around the house, such as washing dishes, sweeping, or raking leaves. Discuss how satisfying it is to complete a task and to feel that you have done a good job.

March 21

"The lazy man is wiser in his own eyes than seven men who can answer sensibly."

—Proverbs 26:16 (NKJV)

Lord, I pray that my grandchild would never be so presumptuous as to think she has all the answers. Please give her a humble spirit and the discipline to look to You for wisdom. Give her understanding of herself and her limitations and the good sense to listen to the counsel of those far wiser than herself.

Application: Share a personal experience about a time when someone gave you some good advice that changed your thinking and action. Reinforce God's directive in Scripture to seek the counsel of those who are wise.

March 22

"He who ignores discipline
comes to poverty and shame,
but whoever heeds correction is honored."

--PROVERBS 13:18

Lord, I ask on behalf of my grandchild for a humble, teachable spirit. Please open his heart and mind to those around him who are older and wiser. Do not let pride and arrogance hinder him from learning from those godly people You have placed in his life to guide him. Help him to emulate their disciplined and faith-filled spirits.

Application: Ask your grandchild, "Who is your hero (or heroine)? Whom do you most admire?" Discuss the people in your local community who have been honored as a result of their hard work and discipline—athletes, musicians, students, etc.

March 23

"I went by the field of the lazy man, and by the vineyard of the man devoid of understanding; and there it was, all overgrown with thorns; its surface was covered with nettles; its stone wall was broken down. When I saw it, I considered it well; I looked on it and received instruction: a little sleep, a little slumber, a little folding of the hands to rest; so shall your poverty come like a prowler, and your need like an armed man."

– Proverbs 24:30-34 (NKJV)

Father, pray that my grandchild would be as wise as the onlooker in this proverb and see the consequences of a lazy life. Help her find the balance between rest and hard work. Let her be disciplined with her time and tasks so that she will not be "robbed" of all that You have for her to enjoy.

Application: Tell your grandchild the story of the grasshopper and the ant. The grasshopper did not prepare for winter and then was rescued by the ant, who had made the necessary preparations and was willing to share.

March 24

"A fool gives full vent to his anger,
but a wise man keeps himself under control."

—Proverbs 29:11

Father, please give my grandchild the discipline to control his emotions. Remind him of Your promise to be his refuge. Bless him with the comfort of knowing that every anxiety and every fear may be poured out before You. May his disciplined life and quiet trust in Your mercy and goodness influence others to turn to You in times of distress.

Application: Share with your grandchild how Jesus provides complete access to the throne of God, where we can pour out every feeling and emotion. Read Psalm 62:8 and assure him that God will take care of him at all times.

March 25

"The soul of the lazy man desires,
and has nothing;
but the soul of the diligent
shall be made rich."

—Proverbs 13:4 (NKJV)

Lord, we live in a culture obsessed with creating discontent through manipulative advertising. Please give my grandchild the wisdom to see through such deception and the ability to guard against discontent. Help her to be industrious in her work and to be satisfied with what You give her. May she have a right understanding of honest labor and its rewards—that those rewards may sometimes be spiritual rather than material.

Application: Look through magazines with your grandchild and discuss how advertisements affect her. Which ads impact her positively? Which impact her negatively?

March 26

"Finish your outdoor work and get your fields ready; after that, build your house."

– Proverbs 24:27

Lord, please enable my grandchild to put his priorities in order. Help him to see how important it is to take care of the necessities of life before indulging in the comforts. I pray that You would give him the discipline required to invest his time and energy in productive work. Also bless him with the wisdom to use his gifts and abilities to further Your kingdom.

Application: Tell your grandchild about your own experience with work. Emphasize the importance of saving for the purchases he needs. Discuss the difference between what we want and what we actually need, as well as helping him learn to prioritize his finances.

March 27

"Do not envy wicked men,
do not desire their company;
for their hearts plot violence,
and their lips talk about making trouble."

— Proverbs 24:1-2

Father, how honest and realistic Your Holy Scriptures are. This proverb warns us of the temptation to be envious of wrongdoers and to pursue evil. I acknowledge, Lord, that there is no way for my grandchild to resist such temptation on her own. Please protect her from wrong companions who might influence her to stray from Your safe and secure path. Help her to live in such a way that she would be disciplined to stay away from evil.

Application: Read the verse above with your grandchild. Point out that God tells us that evil people plot, or plan, to do wrong. As a person of faith, discuss how we can plan to do good in our lives.

March 28

"The lazy man does not roast his game,
but the diligent man prizes his possessions."

— Proverbs 12:27

Lord, You have given us this beautiful world in which to live. It takes work, however, to cultivate the earth and provide for ourselves and our families. Please give my grandchild the diligence and strength of character to work hard. Do not allow him to be lazy or to take Your goodness for granted. As You bless him with the fruit of his labor, I pray that he will not only "prize his possessions," but will generously share them with others.

Application: With your grandchild, plant an herb garden—either inside the house, in pots, or outside. As the herbs grow, share them with your neighbors.

March 29

"He who tends a fig tree will eat its fruit,
and he who looks after his master
will be honored."

—Proverbs 27:18

Lord, thank You for giving us all kinds of interesting work to do in Your world. I am excited and eagerly anticipate watching my grandchild use the aptitudes and talents You have given her for her unique vocation. While we understand that our world is not perfect and that labor can be difficult at times, please enable her to see her work as a positive gift from You. Bless her efforts to be diligent in those areas to which she is called.

Application: Visit a workplace (i.e. fire station, police station, etc.) and discuss the different aptitudes and skills people need to do certain jobs. Affirm for your grandchild that the Lord has a unique design for her life and that using her talents for God's glory will bring her the greatest satisfaction on earth.

March 30

"She makes linen garments and sells them, and supplies the merchants with sashes."

– Proverbs 31:24

Father, the verses in Proverbs 31 speak of a remarkable woman. This verse is an excellent example of creativity and diligent work. I pray that my grandchild would have this same creative and industrious spirit. Please equip the adults in his life to guide and direct him in the development of his interests. Bless him with talents and gifts that will honor You and benefit others.

Application: Engage in some creative activity or craft with your grandchild and talk about his interests and how he might use them to honor God.

March 31

"As iron sharpens iron,
so one man sharpens another."

—Proverbs 27:17

Father, thank You that this proverb suggests that we can be sharper and more disciplined in our faith. We know that Your word is as sharp as a two-edged sword (see Hebrews 4:12) and can give us direction in our decisions. This verse exhorts us to help bring understanding and clarity to each other's lives. I pray that my grandchild would be receptive to the counsel of friends and that she, in turn, would stimulate them to work and good deeds.

Application: Demonstrate to your grandchild how to use a knife or tool sharpener, and discuss how a sharp tool is better than a dull one. Share how some friends cause us to become sharper, or better, and others do not.

MAY MY GRANDCHILD POSSESS...

GRACIOUSNESS

APRIL

April 1

"Even a child is known by his actions,
by whether his conduct is pure and right."

—Proverbs 20:11

Lord, I pray that my grandchild's conduct would be full of grace. I ask, Lord, that he would be kind to the poor, loving to the unlovable, encouraging to the downhearted, and compassionate to those in need. Please help him demonstrate behavior that is pure and right—behavior that reflects Your love. And I ask, Lord, that he would be respected and well-regarded because of his actions.

Application: From construction paper, cut out a heart shape and write the words *Helping Others* down the center. Suggest that your grandchild cut out magazine pictures, showing ways we can help others. Glue the pictures onto the heart.

April 2

"When words are many, sin is not absent,
but he who holds his tongue is wise."

—Proverbs 10:19

Lord, I pray that my grandchild might choose her words carefully and use them wisely. Help her to refrain from idle chatter and to learn when to listen and when to speak. Help her to understand that a few well-chosen words are more effective than rambling on without Your Spirit's leadership.

Application: Watch a television show together. Discuss which words were used in kindness and which words caused pain.

April 3

"Like a madman shooting firebrands
or deadly arrows is a man
who deceives his neighbor
and says, "I was only joking!"

—Proverbs 26:18-19

Lord, our real feelings are often revealed in our actions rather than our words. I pray that my grandchild would not be deceived into thinking that he can act one way and speak another. Please help him live a life of consistency—acting and speaking in unison to glorify You at all times. Let him learn to extend grace and love to those around him in a sincere and heartfelt manner.

Application: Ask your grandchild if someone has ever said something kind to him, yet acted in a mean, spiteful manner. Discuss how this made him feel.

April 4

"Put away perversity from your mouth; keep corrupt talk far from your lips."

—Proverbs 4:24

Lord, it is easy to speak words that can be harmful to others and dishonoring to You. I pray that my grandchild will choose her words to reflect a loving and gracious heart. I ask that she might think before she speaks and that her words will bring healing and wholeness to those around her. Let this practice be a reflection of Your love for her.

Application: Help your grandchild make a list of sayings that can be used to bring glory to God, such as: "Thank You for this day" "Praise You, Lord!" etc. Practice using them together.

April 5

"A friend loves at all times,
and a brother is born for adversity."

—Proverbs 17:17

Father, I pray that my grandchild will develop deep and meaningful friendships throughout his life. I ask, Lord, that he would look to Jesus as his model of unconditional love and commitment. Please allow him the privilege of sharing Your grace and mercy with those closest to him. Help him to be dedicated to others by first dedicating his life to You.

Application: Read John 15:9-17 with your grandchild. Discover together how many different ways Jesus demonstrates that He is our Friend.

April 6

"There are six things the Lord hates, seven that are detestable to him: haughty eyes, a lying tongue, hands that shed innocent blood, a heart that devises wicked schemes, feet that are quick to rush into evil, a false witness who pours out lies and a man who stirs up dissension among brothers."

--Proverbs 6:16–19

Father, this verse speaks clearly about the things You hate. I pray that my grandchild will demonstrate traits that are opposite of each of these characteristics. I pray that she would be humble, truthful, pure, righteous, thoughtful, careful with her words, and a peacemaker. Help her see how Jesus demonstrated all these traits on her behalf. May she learn to live more like Jesus and to honor You graciously at all times.

Application: Read the verse above together. Then talk about the kinds of characteristics God likes. Draw an illustration of someone being thoughtful—such as sharing with others, helping with jobs around the house, etc.

April 7

"The mouth of the righteous
is a fountain of life,
but violence overwhelms
the mouth of the wicked."

—Proverbs 10:11

Lord, I pray that my grandchild will be among the righteous, not the wicked! Help him to understand the power of words so that those he chooses will be full of grace, mercy, and love—a fountain of life to all who hear them. May my grandchild desire most of all to use words that lead others to the very Source of all life, Jesus Christ Himself.

Application: Take your grandchild on a walk in the neighborhood or park to look at a fountain. Discuss the flowing water and how water always cleanses and refreshes. Let your grandchild know that his words can be just like a fountain—giving encouragement and refreshment to others.

April 8

"An unfriendly man pursues selfish ends; he defies all sound judgment."

—Proverbs 18:1

Lord, I pray that my grandchild would be a happy and friendly person. I ask that she would not be selfish in her endeavors, but instead would look out for the interests of others. Help her to understand that good judgment dictates that she benefits from being gracious, merciful, and selfless. Allow her character to be built on the understanding of Your Word and Your love.

Application: Trace your grandchild's hand on a sheet of construction paper. On each of the fingers, write acts of kindness that she can do for friends.

April 9

"Do not forsake your friend and the friend of your father, and do not go to your brother's house when disaster strikes you— better a neighbor nearby than a brother far away."

—Proverbs 27:10

Father, when my grandchild is away from his family because of schooling, work, or ministry, I pray that You would send individuals into his life who would be "as close as family." Help him to graciously accept such situations and bless him with relationships that will strengthen his faith. Above all, remind him that You are his heavenly Father—instantly available and always accessible!

Application: On a piece of construction paper, write this saying: "Friends are our chosen family." Ask your grandchild to cut it into puzzle pieces. As you work the puzzle together, talk about what this means.

April 10

"He who despises his neighbor lacks sense, but a man of understanding keeps silent."

—Proverbs 11:12 (nasb)

Lord, please teach my grandchild to extend grace to her neighbors. I pray that she would not mock or ridicule them, but instead would serve them in love. Help her to understand that You have created each individual with a purpose and place in this world and that You love everyone equally. Help her to know when to speak and when to remain silent and allow Your Spirit to do the talking!

Application: With your grandchild, make a small gift to take to a friend or neighbor in need.

April 11

"The poor man and the oppressor
have this in common:
the LORD gives sight to the eyes of both."

—PROVERBS 29:13

Father, create in my grandchild a true understanding of who he is from Your perspective. He is Your beloved child, created in Your image and designed for a purpose in this life. Yet help him also to know that you have created all people in Your image and, therefore, we should treat them with respect and dignity. Help him to live graciously and to see others as You see them—"precious in Your sight."

Application: Explain to your grandchild that the word *gracious* means "kind, merciful, and compassionate." Choose one way to demonstrate graciousness together—such as volunteering at a local food bank or collecting canned goods for a food drive.

April 12

"He who despises his neighbor sins,
but blessed is he who is kind to the needy."

– Proverbs 14:21

Lord, I pray that my grandchild would enjoy friendly relations with her neighbors. More than that, however, I pray that she would be sensitive to the needy people around her and would extend kindness and help to them. Let the words that she speaks be winsome and full of grace so that others will be drawn to You.

Application: Suggest that your grandchild collect items that are no longer needed at home and help her deliver them to a local charity.

April 13

"He who loves a pure heart
and whose speech is gracious
will have the king for his friend."

—Proverbs 22:11

Father, I ask that You would create in my grandchild a pure heart. Help him to desire holiness and purity. I thank You that gracious speech allows us to make friends readily, possibly even with those who are influential. I pray that my grandchild's life will be blessed with an abundance of faithful and godly friends. But please, Lord, allow him to count as his best Friend the King of Kings and Lord of Lords, Jesus.

Application: Make a heart magnet with your grandchild. Cut out a heart from construction paper and print the words *Speak Kindly* on the front. Glue the heart to a magnetic strip and put it on your refrigerator as a reminder to use our words carefully.

April 14

"People curse the man who hoards grain,
but blessing crowns him
who is willing to sell."

—Proverbs 11:26

Lord, please help my grandchild to be governed by a generous, not a miserly spirit. Help her to know how to provide well for herself and her family, yet at the same time to share graciously with others. I pray that she would have a sense of caring for her community. Allow her to hold loosely to the things of this world and to be willing to trust You to provide for all her needs.

Application: Read Joseph's story in Genesis 41:46-57. Discuss how Joseph listened to God, obeyed His directions, and provided grain for all of Egypt during a famine.

April 15

"A man of many companions
may come to ruin,
but there is a friend
who sticks closer than a brother."

—Proverbs 18:24

Father, I pray that my grandchild would select his friends carefully. Help him to be discerning as he seeks friends who will help him walk more closely and consistently with You. I pray that he would not associate with individuals who would bring him to "ruin" and that he would graciously accept the help of friends when needed. But most of all, Lord, I pray that he would know Jesus as a Friend who "sticks closer than a brother."

Application: Make puppets out of brown lunch bags. Create and enact a short play, using the puppets to demonstrate acts of friendship.

April 16

"The tongue that brings healing
is a tree of life,
but a deceitful tongue
crushes the spirit."

—Proverbs 15:4

Lord, You have shown us that our words truly can bring healing to hurting individuals. I pray that my grandchild will learn to use truthful and affirming words that speak abundant life into broken hearts. I pray that she would be sensitive to the damage deceitful words can cause and that she would choose to honor You in all that she says.

<u>Application:</u> Act out a situation with your grandchild where you play the role of someone whose favorite pet has just died. Talk about words that can be used to bring healing.

April 17

"An inheritance quickly gained at the beginning
will not be blessed at the end."

—Proverbs 20:21

Father, this verse reminds us of the New Testament parable of the Prodigal Son. He received his inheritance early and lost it all by living a disreputable life. I pray that my grandchild will live an honorable life at all times—one that is full of grace and mercy—and that he will not have to learn his lessons the hard way. Help him, day by day, to realize the blessings You give him and to use them to Your glory.

Application: Read the story of the Prodigal Son with your grandchild (see Luke 15:11-32). Discuss the graciousness of the father toward both his sinful sons—the reckless son and the self-righteous son—and how that is an example of God's grace in our own lives.

April 18

"An anxious heart weighs a man down,
but a kind word cheers him up."

—Proverbs 12:25

Lord, I pray that my grandchild will have the opportunity to minister to friends who are hurting, anxious, or distraught. Please teach her how to speak words full of grace and encouragement. Give her the wisdom to know how to cheer others through Your Word. And, in turn, Lord, when she is anxious or overwhelmed by circumstances, please bring people into her life who will offer hope and support and remind her to lean on You.

Application: Help your grandchild memorize this proverb so that she can use "a kind word" to help herself and others in difficult times.

April 19

"Do not gloat when your enemy falls;
when he stumbles,
do not let your heart rejoice."

—Proverbs 24:17

Father, I pray that my grandchild would avoid the curse of comparison. Please keep him from taking pleasure in seeing others fall because it makes him look better. Help him resist the temptation to "rejoice" when someone fails, even if it's his worst enemy. I ask instead, Lord, that he would keep his eyes on You and seek to graciously demonstrate Your love to all.

Application: Read Matthew 5:43-45a with your grandchild. Talk about what Jesus meant when He commanded us to love our enemies.

April 20

"Pleasant words are a honeycomb,
sweet to the soul
and healing to the bones."

—Proverbs 16:24

Father, what an amazing concept this proverb presents. "Pleasant words" are not only gratifying to hear, but they can actually bring health to our bodies. I ask on behalf of my grandchild, Lord, that her words would be sweet as well as sincere. I pray that her conversations would be full of grace, used to restore health and vitality to others.

Application: Discuss with your grandchild how words might give health to our bodies—alleviate worry, eliminate loneliness, bring comfort, etc. Most importantly, show how the words we choose can communicate how much God cares about us.

April 21

"A kindhearted woman gains respect,
but ruthless men gain only wealth."

—Proverbs 11:16

Father, in this world it is tempting to believe that material wealth is more valuable than wealth of character. I pray that my grandchild would be kindhearted, compassionate, gracious, and generous so that he would be respected. Help him to understand that the reputation of his character is more important than all the worldly goods he might accumulate.

Application: Share with your grandchild the story of someone you respect because of his or her character and how that person has influenced you.

April 22

"Through patience a ruler can be persuaded, and a gentle tongue can break a bone."

—Proverbs 25:15

Father, persuasion usually involves logical thought and articulate expression. Strangely enough, however, this proverb tells us that persuasion can be the result of patience and gentleness. It also reminds us that gracious and kind words can be just as powerful as ruthless action. I pray that my grandchild would learn these truths and be able to apply them at the appropriate time.

Application: Describe an incident when someone you know broke a bone. Was it the result of a fall? An accident? A fight? This proverb tells us that "a gentle tongue can break a bone." Talk about what this really means: Kind and gentle words can be so powerful that they make a difference in how someone feels, thinks, or acts.

April 23

"A fool shows his annoyance at once,
but a prudent man overlooks an insult."

—Proverbs 12:16

Father, I pray that You would guard my grandchild's temperament. I ask, Lord, that You would help him to be wise, understanding, and prudent. Help him to be a responsive and not a reactive individual. Help him to know when to walk away from an insult and when to respond. Allow any response he may have to be a reflection of Your love.

Application: Discuss with your grandchild how to respond when someone says something mean to you or insults you. Practice "overlooking an insult" by thinking of some "soft answers" (see Proverbs 15:1).

April 24

"Remove the dross from the silver,
and out comes material for the silversmith."

—PROVERBS 25:4

Lord, all of Your children need to go through the process of refinement. I know my grandchild will be no different. But I do pray, Father, for Your hand of protection on her throughout the process. And I ask that You provide her with a spirit of graciousness so that she is willing to receive Your work of sanctification in her life. Afterward, Lord, may she shine like silver!

Application: Read this proverb to your grandchild and explain the meaning of *dross*. Explain how removing the dross from silver is similar to the process God uses to refine us. He makes us more like Him by purifying us and conforming us to Christ through sanctification.

April 25

"Through the blessing of the upright
a city is exalted,
but by the mouth of the wicked
it is destroyed."

—Proverbs 11:11

Father, help my grandchild to bless others with every word he speaks. Help him to be kind, loving, merciful, and gracious. Encourage him to pray for those around him and to be a beacon of Your love in his neighborhood, his city, his country, and the world by the way he lives and the things he says.

Application: Help your grandchild make a list of the important people in his life. Pray with him for God's blessing on each one.

April 26

"He who oppresses the poor shows
contempt for their Maker,
but whoever is kind to the needy
honors God."

—Proverbs 14:31

Father, I pray that my grandchild would honor You by showing compassion and kindness to those in need. I pray that she would not overlook opportunities to do good, but would find many ways to reach out and bless others. Allow her the privilege of sharing Your grace and speaking of her faith so that those she helps would see You as the source of her graciousness and would give You the glory.

Application: Make cookies for a shut-in neighbor or nursing home resident. Help your grandchild deliver them with a note, assuring the shut-in of your love and prayers.

April 27

"Do not exploit the poor
because they are poor
and do not crush the needy in court,
for the Lord will take up their case
and will plunder those who plunder them."

—Proverbs 22:22-23

Lord, Your prophet Isaiah tells us that You are a "refuge for the poor and a refuge for the needy in his distress" (25:4). I pray that my grandchild would never take advantage of another person because he is poor. Help him to honor others by graciously extending Your love and mercy and only desiring what is good and right for all people.

Application: Make a mural entitled "Acts of Kindness." Tape a large sheet of white paper to a wall. Help your grandchild draw scenes depicting different acts of kindness. Then discuss what he has drawn and how he can bring the mural "to life."

April 28

"A kind man benefits himself,
but a cruel man brings trouble on himself."

—Proverbs 11:17

Lord, this proverb reminds us of the beatitude that says: "Blessed are the merciful, for they will be shown mercy" (Matthew 5:7). We reap what we sow. I pray that You would give my grandchild a heart full of mercy, grace, and kindness. And, in turn, Lord, I ask that these very same blessings would return to her a hundred-fold.

Application: Discuss the concept of "random acts of kindness" and what that might mean. Introduce the phrase "redemptive acts of kindness." These would be kind deeds done to demonstrate and share the gospel. Talk about how you can quietly and anonymously do kind deeds for others to help them learn about Jesus. Then choose and complete a "redemptive act of kindness" together.

April 29

"The righteous hate what is false,
but the wicked bring shame and disgrace."

--Proverbs 13:5

Father, I pray that my grandchild would learn to hate lies as much as You do! I ask that he will love what is right, true, and pure. Create in him a character that would not bring shame and disgrace, but instead would bring honor. May his family, community, and You, his Lord, be honored by his respectful and gracious nature.

Application: With your grandchild, make a "badge of honor" out of cardboard. Help him decorate it, then pin it on him. Discuss how a life of honor would be characterized by kind words, thoughtful actions, and brave deeds.

April 30

"He who conceals his hatred has lying lips, and whoever spreads slander is a fool."

—Proverbs 10:18

Lord, we can try to hide our hatred with flattery and our jealousy with slander. We know, however, that we cannot hide anything from You. You know our hearts, our intentions, and our true thoughts. I pray that my grandchild's speech would be full of grace, overflowing from a heart full of love for You.

Application: Share this quote with your grandchild and discuss its implications: "Gossip is what you say behind someone's back that you would never say to their face. Flattery is what you say to someone's face that you would never say behind their back." (Pastor Wilson Benton, CPC, Nashville, TN)

MAY MY GRANDCHILD SHOW...

Generosity

MAY

May 1

"Honor the LORD with your wealth,
with the first fruits of all your crops;
then your barns will be filled to overflowing,
and your vats will brim over
with new wine."

—PROVERBS 3:9-10

Lord, Your Word commands that we honor You with our "first fruits," not with the leftovers of our resources, time, and talents. Develop in my grandchild the heart of a generous giver and allow her to experience the joy of giving from her earliest days. Thank You for promising to bless her with abundance as she gives back to You.

Application: Share how you give to the Lord and His work from what He has given you. For example, talk about tithing to your church, giving to a mission organization or world hunger effort, etc. Then tell your grandchild how the Lord has blessed you for your obedience.

May 2

"Love and faithfulness keep a king safe; through love his throne is made secure."

– Proverbs 20:28

Lord, this proverb states that love and faithfulness bring safety. A king is safer when he loves and is faithful to his people. A child is safer when he experiences the love and faithfulness of his parents. We are all safe in Your arms when we know Your love. Such abundant love comes from a heart of generosity. Help my grandchild to experience Your generous love and to be generous in loving others. Help him to know the safety of unconditional love and to stay very close to You all of his life.

Application: Draw a small circle in the middle of a piece of paper and put your grandchild's name in it. Then draw a series of connected circles around the inner circle. In each of those connected circles, write the name of someone who loves him. Discuss how safe it feels to be surrounded by people who love us.

May 3

"She opens her arms to the poor and extends her hands to the needy."

—Proverbs 31:20

Father, I thank You for the reminder throughout Your Word that we are to care for the poor and needy. I pray that my grandchild would proactively reach out with a heart of compassion. Please give her an ability not only to empathize with those in need, but to be generous with her resources—spiritual, physical, and material.

Application: Read James 2:1-4 and discuss with your grandchild how the Bible says we should show no partiality in our treatment of others.

May 4

"A man finds joy in giving an apt reply –
and how good is a timely word!"

– Proverbs 15:23

Lord, we know that generosity involves much more than the giving of goods and services. Thank You for reminding my grandchild that when he offers someone a word of wisdom, knowledge, or comfort at an appropriate time, he both gives and receives a blessing. Help him to always communicate with kindness as a demonstration of Your love.

Application: Using a small hour glass, have a contest to see how many encouraging words you can think of in a short time.

May 5

"The prospect of the righteous is joy,
but the hopes of the wicked
come to nothing."

—Proverbs 10:28

Father, thank You that my grandchild can look forward to a joyful and abundant future if she walks in Your ways. Help her, Lord, as she lives her faith to be generous and loving. May she recognize that only a hope founded in You will bring joy, both now and for eternity.

Application: Teach your grandchild the short song: "I've got the joy, joy, joy, joy down in my heart, down in my heart, down in my heart. I've got the joy, joy, joy, joy down in my heart to stay." Explain that the joy in our hearts is there because of all that God has done for us. The outcome should be hearts overflowing with generosity to others!

May 6

"Open your mouth for the dumb (those unable to speak for themselves), for the rights of all who are left desolate and defenseless. Open your mouth, judge righteously, and administer justice for the poor and needy."

– Proverbs 31:8-9 (the amplified bible)

Father, help my grandchild faithfully apply these verses in his life. Please give him the ability and courage to speak out on behalf of all those who are helpless to defend themselves. May his life be characterized by a generous spirit that is always attentive to the needs of the poor and is willing to make sure that there is justice for the needy.

Application: Discuss the difficulties that newcomers to a country might have when they cannot speak the language. As an example, share some things your grandchild might do to help such a new student in his class at school.

May 7

"Such is the end of all who go after ill-gotten gain; it takes away the lives of those who get it."

—Proverbs 1:19

Lord, this is a sobering verse for those of us tempted by the wealth and materialism of this world. Accumulating too much "stuff" is a common failing in our culture; eventually, as this proverb indicates, the things we own can own us! Please help my grandchild value those things which bring contentment and are of eternal value. Bless her with hands that grip your earthly blessings loosely so that she might give generously to others.

Application: Finger paint with your grandchild and make hand prints of many different colors. Discuss how we need to be open-handed with what we have so that we can generously share with others.

May 8

"For a man's ways are in full view of the LORD, and he examines all his paths."

—PROVERBS 5:21

Lord, because You are omniscient, we know that everything we think, say, and do is performed right before Your eyes. I pray that my grandchild would be mindful that You are watching—not to condemn, but to correct and encourage. Please work in his heart in such a way that he will choose the path of generosity and be able to further Your kingdom work.

Application: Take a walk up a hill with your grandchild and show him how that vantage point allows him a full view of the countryside. Share how God's view is so much greater—He sees and knows everything and is always watching over us.

May 9

"The righteous care about justice for the poor, but the wicked have no such concern."

—Proverbs 29:7

Lord, a righteous person follows Your word in all that she does. I pray that my grandchild would be such a person. According to this proverb, she will then care about assuring justice for the poor. I pray that she will be generous with her possessions, her time, and her efforts as she seeks equality for all people. Help her actions to continually reflect Your heart and Your love.

Application: Talk about a specific way in which poor people suffer. Think of one method to help change their situation. For example, a poor person might not be able to pay his utility bills. Suggest that your grandchild contribute to a fund that will help pay those bills.

May 10

"He who oppresses the poor to increase his wealth and he who gives gifts to the rich—both come to poverty."

—Proverbs 22:16

Father, thank You for the wise counsel found in this proverb concerning our relationship with both the rich and the poor. Please help my grandchild learn to be honest and ethical in his dealings with all people. May he be known for his generosity to those in need and his sincerity toward those who are wealthy. Please help him remember not to oppress the poor or curry the favor of the rich and always to be thankful for the sufficiency found in You.

Application: Research a world hunger organization, such as World Vision, Food for the Hungry, or Heifer International. Discuss the many ways to help others and decide on one you and your grandchild can participate in together.

May 11

"Like clouds and wind without rain
is a man who boasts of gifts
he does not give."

– Proverbs 25:14

Father, this verse reminds me that we are to be true to our word at all times. May my grandchild not pledge to give things she cannot deliver. Help her to be generous with gifts when possible, but realistic in what she promises. May she be grateful for the gifts and blessings she has received from You.

Application: Discuss with your grandchild how it would feel to be promised a big gift (a trip to Disneyworld, a new car, a favorite toy) and then not receive it. What would she think of the person who promised the gift? Is this true generosity?

May 12

"Like cold water to a weary soul
is good news
from a distant land."

—Proverbs 25:25

Lord, it is easy to become discouraged when one is far away. School, jobs, marriage, or a call to missions may separate us from those we love and care about. I pray that my grandchild would often remember those who may not be near and then be willing to send kind words, cheering thoughts, and heartfelt prayers. May he be generous with his time and efforts as he shares good news and brings hope to the weary.

Application: Write a letter of encouragement to someone in another part of the world—a missionary, soldier, friend, etc.

May 13

"Do not withhold good
from those who deserve it,
when it is in your power to act."

—Proverbs 3:27

Lord, I pray that You will give my grandchild the desire to bless deserving people when the opportunity arises. Help her to remember the Golden Rule and to do the good things for others that she would want others to do for her. Empower her by Your Spirit, because without You, she can accomplish nothing.

Application: Help your grandchild memorize the Golden Rule from Luke 6:31: "Do to others as you would have them do to you."

May 14

"The crown of the wise is their riches,
but the foolishness of fools is folly."

—Proverbs 14:24 (NKJV)

Father, a crown made of sparkling jewels is a beautiful object to behold, but how much more beautiful is a crown of wisdom. Please enable my grandchild to distinguish between these two crowns. Help him understand his position as a child of the King and desire to please You by living a life of generosity and wisdom.

Application: Allow your grandchild to be king for a day. Discuss ways that he could be a kind and generous king.

May 15

"If your enemy is hungry, give him food to eat; if he is thirsty, give him water to drink."

—Proverbs 25:21

Lord, I pray that my grandchild would have Your power to love even those who may be her enemies. This may mean that she is kind when she would like to be hurtful, or generous when she feels like being stingy. It could mean that she would share something with someone when she really wants to keep it for herself. In this way, she will overcome evil with good, and You will be glorified.

Application: Read the story of the Good Samaritan (see Luke 10:25-37) and discuss with your grandchild how the Samaritan man showed kindness to his enemy.

May 16

"A gift opens the way for the giver
and ushers him into
the presence of the great."

—Proverbs 18:16

Father, thank You that Your Word reveals that the gifts You have given my grandchild may usher him before the "greats" of this world. In so doing, You will give him opportunities to tell about Your grace and love. Thank You most of all for the greatest Gift of all—Your Son, Jesus Christ. Help my grandchild to receive that most precious Gift and discover Your plan for his life.

<ins>Application:</ins> Read John 1:12 together: "Yet to all who received him, to those who believed in His name, he gave the right to become children of God." Discuss how God wants us to receive His gift of Jesus and become part of His family.

May 17

"A generous man will prosper;
he who refreshes others
will himself be refreshed."

—Proverbs 11:25

Lord, we often think of refreshment in the form of food and drink. This proverb, however, reminds us that Your description of refreshment involves generosity. I pray that my grandchild would develop a generous heart and, therefore, would experience the spiritual refreshment that comes through blessing people. May her life prosper in faith and friendship as she ministers to family, classmates, and others.

Application: Refresh yourselves with a glass of lemonade and talk about how God loves us and generously blesses us in so many ways.

May 18

"Do not say, `I'll do to him as
he has done to me;
I'll pay that man back for what he did.'"

– Proverbs 24:29

Lord, sometimes it is difficult not to want to take revenge on those who have treated us unfairly. I pray that You would give my grandchild a heart like Yours, one that is generous with forgiveness. Help him to know that ultimately You will deliver justice to all mankind and that he can trust You when he is hurt. Instead of repaying evil for evil, may his heart and mind be focused on "turning the other cheek" and doing what is good.

Application: Read 1 Peter 3:9 to your grandchild: "Do not repay evil with evil or insult with insult, but with blessing, because to this you were called so that you may inherit a blessing." Talk about the fact that many times the Bible asks us to do things that seem hard, but they are the right thing to do.

May 19

"One man gives freely, yet gains even more;
another withholds unduly,
but comes to poverty."

—Proverbs 11:24

Lord, it has been said that we can never out-give You. Your economic principles regarding giving are so very different from the world's view. I pray that my grandchild will learn early that the more she gives, the more she will receive! I also pray that my grandchild would not withhold any of her resources, but would be eager to share them with those in need.

Application: Read the story of the loaves and the fishes to your grandchild (see Mark 6:35–44). Talk about what happened when a young boy shared his dinner with Jesus.

May 20

"As water reflects a face,
so a man's heart reflects the man."

—Proverbs 27:19

Lord, You have generously blessed my grandchild. I pray that his life would be an expression of your abundant provision and a demonstration of your faithfulness. May his heart also be one of a "generous man [who] devises generous things" (Isaiah 32:8a NKJV*). Help him to understand that as water or a mirror reflects his outer image, his heart will reflect his inner character, which I pray will be a reflection of You as his faith grows.*

Application: Show your grandchild his reflection in water or in a mirror and talk about outward appearances versus inward character.

May 21

"Rescue those being led away to death;
hold back those
staggering toward slaughter."

—PROVERBS 24:11

Lord, I pray that my grandchild would be generous in her love and compassion for others. Make her an advocate for those who cannot speak for themselves—the unborn, the disadvantaged, and the oppressed. We know, however, that the true Advocate is Jesus Christ, who lived and died on our behalf so that we might have eternal life. May my grandchild's generosity include sharing the good news of Jesus with others who need a Rescuer.

Application: Help your grandchild make a list of all of her unsaved friends and family members. Pray together for the salvation of those individuals who do not know Jesus as their Savior.

May 22

"He who is kind to the poor
lends to the LORD,
and he will reward him
for what he has done."

—PROVERBS 19:17

Father, I thank You that when my grandchild extends kindness to the poor, he has the promise of a reward. And how amazing that when he blesses those who are less fortunate, he is actually giving to You! I pray that Your Holy Spirit will develop in him a generous and kind heart toward all people. Please let him know that he is especially pleasing to You when he demonstrates a lifestyle of giving to the poor.

Application: Decorate a jar to use for collecting coins. Put spare change in the jar. When it is full, contribute to the church benevolence fund or decide together how you should give the money away.

May 23

"A stingy man is eager to get rich and is unaware that poverty awaits him."

— Proverbs 28:22

Father, this verse reminds us that greed often leads to an impoverished life. I pray that my grandchild would not be stingy, but would choose to be generous. Help her know that You promise blessings as she shares her resources (see Malachi 3:10). I pray that the motives of my grandchild's heart will reflect Your love and that she will use her gifts for Your glory.

Application: Talk about the character Scrooge in *A Christmas Carol* by Charles Dickens. Scrooge was a stingy man whose heart was transformed one Christmas.

May 24

"The blessing of the LORD brings wealth, and he adds no trouble to it."

—PROVERBS 10:22

Father, we understand that "wealth" can take a variety of forms. I ask on behalf of my grandchild for a heart that is rich toward You. Focus his mind on an eternal inheritance which can never rust or be stolen. Please show him how to use Your many blessings to benefit others.

Application: Read Matthew 6:19-21 with your grandchild. Discuss how the Bible says we need to store up treasures in heaven. Explain that as he generously uses what the Lord has given him, he will continue to see God's blessings.

May 25

"If a man shuts his ears to the cry of the poor, he too will cry out and not be answered."

--Proverbs 21:13

Father, this proverb is a reminder that whatever we sow on this earth will be what we reap (see Galatians 6:7). I pray that You would help my grandchild to have open ears to the "cry of the poor." Help her to generously share her resources in whatever ways You lead her. Thank You that as she is attentive to others, You will be glorified and her own needs will be met.

<u>Application</u>: Demonstrate the principle of reaping and sowing. Plant two pots of seed; water and fertilize one and neglect the other. Watch the results!

May 26

"He who gives to the poor will lack nothing,
but he who closes his eyes to them
receives many curses."

--Proverbs 28:27

Lord, You tell us that as we share with the poor, we will never be in need. Help my grandchild to be sensitive to those around him. Let him not be indifferent to the impoverished or the disenfranchised. Help my grandchild to be quick to share, knowing his reward is from You.

Application: Help your grandchild clean out a closet and then take the unneeded clothes to an organization or shelter that supports the poor.

May 27

"Those who plan what is good
find love and faithfulness."

—Proverbs 14:22b

Lord, there are so many choices in our lives. We can choose to follow You or to reject You. We can choose to be faithful or to be rebellious. We can be generous or stingy. We can be kind or hateful. Help my grandchild, Lord, to make good choices in her life and to live a life of faithfulness, kindness, and generosity.

Application: Read together Luke 19:1-9. Talk about the biblical character Zacchaeus and how generous he became after meeting the Lord.

May 28

"A gift given in secret
soothes anger."

—Proverbs 21:14a

Father, thank You for Your wise counsel that an unexpected gift can soothe anger and redeem a contentious situation. Help my grandchild to be unselfish in difficult circumstances and to be willing to generously give a gift to quiet an angry spirit. Let him see that this gift could be a kind word or a helpful act, just as well as a material gift. Help him to know what an instrument of peace a gift might be and how it can help refocus on joy.

Application: Find someone in a difficult situation and encourage your grandchild to offer a word of hope, a kind act, or a material gift. Suggest that the gift be given anonymously so that only God receives the glory.

May 29

"A generous man will himself be blessed, for he shares his food with the poor."

—Proverbs 22:9

Lord, over and over again in Your Word, we find that You stir our consciences regarding the poor. Your heart is so big and so compassionate, and I thank You that my grandchild is created in Your image! Please stir her creativity to seek even more ways to provide for those who are hungry. Help her understand her responsibility as Your child to share what she has received from Your generous hand.

Application: Demonstrate sharing by inviting to dinner someone who is experiencing financial difficulty—a job layoff, illness, debt—and is not expected to return the invitation. Let your grandchild set the table or otherwise help to prepare for your guest.

May 30

"He who plots evil
will be known as a schemer."

—Proverbs 24:8

Lord, thank You that Your Word helps us to consider how our thoughts affect our actions. For example, if we focus on plotting evil, we will be more likely to carry out evil schemes. Therefore, I pray that my grandchild would focus on ways to be good and generous, such as showing hospitality or serving his community. Please allow him to see how he can benefit others rather than how they can benefit him. May his motives be pure as he seeks to follow You, the only One who is truly good.

Application: With your grandchild, devise a plan to be generous to someone in need. This may mean giving a gift, doing a good deed, or inviting someone over for a meal.

May 31

"Do not say to your neighbor,
'Come back later: I'll give it tomorrow'
when you now have it with you."

—Proverbs 3:28

Lord, help my grandchild to be sensitive to the concerns of others at all times. I pray that she would be known as a trustworthy person as she fulfills her obligations. May she even go beyond what is required and be generous in sharing her time, gifts, and talents.

Application: Ask your grandchild to complete a task for you and promise a particular reward in return—stickers, money, etc. When the task is completed, double the reward, and help your grandchild understand that generosity is extended when you give more that is required of you.

MAY MY GRANDCHILD DISPLAY...

HUMILITY

JUNE

June 1

"The LORD detests all the proud of heart.
Be sure of this:
They will not go unpunished."

—PROVERBS 16:5

Lord, You are the Creator of every person who has ever lived on this planet. I pray that You would give my grandchild the ability to see himself rightly in relation to You and never think more highly of himself than he ought. Please give him a spirit of humility that can only come as he understands all that is his through the finished work of Christ. May his only "boast" be in the cross of Jesus.

Application: Discuss with your grandchild how difficult it is sometimes to say you are sorry. The root of this difficulty is pride—believing that you are right and should not have to compromise or change.

June 2

"Do not fret because of evil men
or be envious of the wicked,
for the evil man has no future hope,
and the lamp of the wicked
will be snuffed out."

—Proverbs 24:19-20

Lord, this verse is a reminder of how easily our thoughts can turn from trust and thankfulness to fear and envy. I pray that my grandchild's heart and mind would be centered on You. Please help her to be grateful for the circumstances You allow in her life that cause her to humbly turn to You for guidance and protection.

<ins>Application:</ins> Light a candle and have your grandchild extinguish the flame with a candle snuffer. Explain how God will not allow the light of wicked people to continue, but His light, His Word, and His plans will prevail.

June 3

"My son, if you have put up security for your neighbor, if you have struck hands in pledge for another, if you have been trapped by what you said, ensnared by the words of your mouth, then do this, my son, to free yourself, since you have fallen into your neighbor's hands; go and humble yourself; press your plea with your neighbor!"

—Proverbs 6:1-3

Father, there will be times when my grandchild will experience difficult relationships because he has not been wise in his choice of words. Help him to see clearly his mistakes and give him the courage to confess his wrongdoing. May he understand that You promise to use his weakness to demonstrate Your strength (see 2 Corinthians 12:10).

Application: Share a story where your words and actions entangled you in a difficult situation and required you to humble yourself before someone else.

June 4

"A man's own folly ruins his life,
yet his heart rages against the LORD."

—PROVERBS 19:3

Father, it is often our own choices that bring ruin and disaster. Yet so often we blame another person... or even You. I pray that the heart of my grandchild would be full of gratitude and not rage. I ask that she would surrender her will to Yours and invite Your direction and guidance. Help her to welcome the work You can do in her life.

Application: Read the story of "Jack and the Beanstalk" to your grandchild. Explain how the giant fell to his destruction after losing his temper.

June 5

"Let another praise you,
and not your own mouth;
someone else, and not your own lips."

—Proverbs 27:2

Father, You are so gracious to give Your people such wise counsel for living. None of us enjoys being around a person who is constantly praising himself. Help my grandchild to do his work without boasting or drawing attention to himself. May he come to understand that accepting praise from others and, ultimately, from You, is of much more value than reciting his accomplishments.

Application: Talk to your grandchild about how he can praise and encourage others. Then make a list of positive comments he can pass along to a parent or loved one: "Thank you for your care," "I appreciate your help," "I love you," etc.

June 6

"To fear the LORD is to hate evil;
I hate pride and arrogance,
evil behavior and perverse speech."

—PROVERBS 8:13

Father, as Your people, we are called to be like You, loving what You love and hating what You hate. Thank You for being so specific about what is important to You. I pray that the Holy Spirit would enlighten my grandchild in such a way that she will be able to discern good from evil and will humbly submit to His guidance as He leads her into all truth and righteousness.

Application: With your grandchild, make a collage of pictures cut from a magazine. Choose pictures of some things God loves and some He hates. Discuss the difference.

June 7

"A greedy man brings trouble to his family, but he who hates bribes will live."

--Proverbs 15:27

Father, You know the temptations of the world faced by Your people. Please strengthen my grandchild to resist any worldly attraction which would divert him from a walk of faith. Help him not to be greedy. Instead, help him to be satisfied with living honestly, recognizing that You alone are sufficient to meet all his needs.

Application: Explain the definition of a bribe to your grandchild. Then discuss the trouble that is caused when bribes are involved. For instance, if a politician is paid to vote a certain way (bribery), that might result in a beneficial law failing to pass.

June 8

"He who conceals his sins does not prosper,
but whoever confesses
and renounces them finds mercy."

—Proverbs 28:13

Father, thank You for being the God of all grace and mercy. Please help my grandchild to recognize her wrong behavior and to be quick to confess and repent. In humility, help her to turn to You for forgiveness. Create in her a heart that is grateful for Your mercy, rejoices in Your love, and celebrates her relationship with You.

Application: Read Luke 7:36-50 together and experience the joy and celebration of a woman who was forgiven of her sins and received the acceptance and love of the Lord.

June 9

"When a wicked man dies,
his hope perishes;
all he expected from his power
comes to nothing."

—Proverbs 11:7

Lord, as our Father, You have prepared an inheritance in heaven which will never perish. Thank You that my grandchild can experience hope here on earth—not because of what he has done, but because of all that Jesus has done in his behalf. Please give him the ability to see day-to-day events from an eternal perspective and to be grateful that Your invisible hand is working all things together for his good and Your glory.

Application: Discuss with your grandchild how God's hand was involved in his unique design—even down to his fingerprints! Using finger paint and construction paper, make a print of your grandchild's hand, glue a magnet to the back, and mount it on the fridge.

June 10

"Humility and the fear of the LORD bring wealth and honor and life."

—PROVERBS 22:4

Father, thank You for this wonderful promise of reward to those who humbly trust in You. Please give my grandchild the discernment to accept the time and place of these rewards. Help her to gratefully receive Your blessings here on earth and to patiently await those rewards to be enjoyed in heaven. Whatever Your plan for her life, may her primary focus be not on the gifts she receives, but on the Giver.

Application: Tell your grandchild the story of Joseph from Genesis 37-47. Relate how Joseph had to humble himself many times and how he feared the Lord rather than man. The result was wealth, honor, and life—not only for himself, but for all of Israel.

June 11

"The LORD tears down
the proud man's house,
but he keeps the widow's
boundaries intact."

—PROVERBS 15:25

Lord, we acknowledge You as the supreme Sovereign over all creation, full of power and glory. We are also amazed by your tenderness and compassion toward those—like the widow in this proverb—who are most helpless and needy. I pray that you will give my grandchild a heart of humility that overflows with love for those deemed by the world to be unworthy. Please help him to see how much You have given him and make him eager to share with others.

Application: With your grandchild, prepare food or a special treat for a widow or needy person. Deliver the gift and share about the good things God has been doing in your life.

June 12

"A cheerful heart is good medicine,
but a crushed spirit dries up the bones."

—Proverbs 17:22

Father, this passage indicates to us that our inner condition can affect our physical health. Because a cheerful heart is good medicine, I pray that You would give my grandchild a heart overflowing with joy and gratitude. Please allow her spirit to be alive with Your love. May she find comfort in Your soothing presence during any illness or disappointment. Finally, let her rejoice in Your love that will never let her go.

Application: Discuss with your grandchild the different types of medications to cure diseases and keep us healthy. God has provided doctors who can give us medicine to treat illness, but God can also "give medicine" by cheering a humble heart with His joy.

June 13

"A man's pride brings him low,
but a man of lowly spirit gains honor."

—Proverbs 29:23

Lord, we acknowledge that You alone are worthy of our worship and praise. I know You have gifted my grandchild with talents and abilities to be used for Your glory. I pray that these would not make him prideful, but that he would humbly use them as a tribute to You. If others honor him for his accomplishments, may he, in turn, deflect that honor and praise to You.

Application: Help your grandchild to show his gratitude for someone who uses his gifts to honor God—a pastor, a priest, a Sunday school teacher—by writing a note of thanks, giving a small gift, drawing a picture, etc.

June 14

"He mocks proud mockers,
but gives grace to the humble."

—Proverbs 3:34

Lord, we praise You that You "dwell in the high and holy place," yet You also abide "with him who has a contrite and humble spirit" (Isaiah 57:15 NKJV*). What an awesome God You are! I pray that Your Holy Spirit would "dwell" (take up residence) in my grandchild and give her a spirit of gratitude and humility. Please pour out Your grace upon her as she lives a life of humble obedience.*

Application: Practice bowing or curtsying as you would if you were meeting the Queen of England. Share how this is a demonstration of respect and humility, acknowledging the queen's position of authority. How much more awed and respectful we should be when coming before the King of the universe, who created us and loves and sustains us.

June 15

"Do not exalt yourself in the king's presence,
and do not claim a place among great men;
it is better for him to say to you,
`Come up here,' than for him to humiliate
you before a nobleman."

—Proverbs 25:6-7a

Father, Jesus used this verse to teach about humility when he described how guests at a wedding feast often chose the places of honor for themselves (see Luke 14:7-11). I pray that You would give my grandchild humility and a heart to serve others. May his motivation never be to exalt himself, but to exalt You and to put others first.

Application: Teach your grandchild good table manners that demonstrate respect and service toward others. Practice good manners by having a "tea party" or "cookie and milk party" together.

June 16

"A happy heart makes the face cheerful,
but heartache crushes the spirit."

—Proverbs 15:13

Father, we see two very different attitudes of the heart in this proverb and the reality that one's disposition on the inside will eventually determine what is observed on the outside. Help my grandchild to humbly seek the joy that only Jesus can give; may that joy be reflected in her countenance. Please enable her to understand that You can use something as simple as her compassionate smile in the work of Your kingdom.

Application: Decorate smiley-face cookies with your grandchild and talk about the many cheerful and joyful friends for whom you are thankful.

June 17

"When pride comes, then comes disgrace, but with humility comes wisdom."

—Proverbs 11:2

Father, thank You for not leaving Your people to wonder what true humility looks like. Jesus has shown us how to be humble. I pray that my grandchild would always seek to imitate the manner and method of Jesus and that he would know that only Your Holy Spirit can give him the power to live a Christ-like life. May he understand that as he humbly submits every aspect of his life to You that he will gain true wisdom.

Application: Discuss with your grandchild how Jesus exhibited humility and submission when He willingly left the glories of heaven and became a human being (John 17:5).

June 18

"Death and Destruction are never satisfied, and neither are the eyes of man."

– Proverbs 27:20

Lord, knowing the human heart better than we do, You know that it is never satisfied. I pray that You would enable my grandchild to see the pride of her own heart with its subtle desire for more. Give her the ability to be content with the life You have given her. Please help her, Father, to know that her longings can never be satisfied apart from the love of Jesus.

Application: Look through a catalogue with your grandchild. Discuss how we are never satisfied with the latest "thing" and are always looking for the next and newest.

June 19

"It is better to be of a humble spirit
with the lowly,
than to divide the spoil
with the proud."

—Proverbs 16:19 (nasb)

Father, thank You for the way Jesus lived out this proverb so perfectly. He associated with people of all walks of life, from the greatest to the least. Please help my grandchild choose to be like Jesus and to desire to spend time with humble people. I pray that the temporary riches of this world would not entice him. Instead, make him content to be with others who are grateful, faithful, and righteous.

Application: Introduce your grandchild to someone who is involved with ministry—a Sunday school teacher, pastor, inner-city minister—and exemplifies a humble spirit.

June 20

"Locusts have no king,
yet they advance together in ranks."

—Proverbs 30:27

Lord, Your plan and order are exhibited in the life patterns of some of Your smallest creatures. Please give my grandchild the ability to learn important lessons in humility from even such insects as the locusts. Help her to see how great things are accomplished when people are willing to submit to each other for Your purposes. I pray, Father, that You would give her the desire to cooperate and work with others to advance Your kingdom.

Application: Teach your grandchild about locusts, using reference books or the Internet. Discuss the devastating power of locusts when they unite in a swarm. Compare the power for good available to God's people when they come together and pool their time, talents, and resources.

June 21

"All the days of the oppressed are wretched,
but the cheerful heart
has a continual feast."

—Proverbs 15:15

Father, You have created us with minds and hearts that respond to Your work in our lives. Please give my grandchild the desire to study Your Word so that he might humbly view his life from Your perspective. Please protect him from the cynicism of the world and bless him with a cheerful heart that reflects Your love. Help him to be grateful for the joy that only a relationship with You can bring.

Application: Make a chain of hearts out of construction paper and write "cheerful" words on each heart. A chain can be made by accordion-folding red construction paper, drawing the heart out from the fold, and cutting along the shape lines, but not along the fold. (More specific directions can be found at http:kabubble.com/ac_heart_chain.html).

June 22

"A proud and arrogant man—
'Scoffer' is his name;
he acts with arrogant pride."

—Proverbs 21:24 (NKJV)

Father, names can sometimes be an indication of a person's character (see 1 Samuel 25:25). You know how precious the name of my grandchild is to me. Help her to see that she is even more precious to You. Draw her by Your love into Your family. Please work in her life in such a way that, at the sound of her name, people would be drawn—not to her, but to You.

Application: Look up the meaning of your grandchild's name in a baby's name book found at a bookstore, library, or online. Talk about how your grandchild received her name.

June 23

"A cheerful look brings joy to the heart, and good news gives health to the bones."

—Proverbs 15:30

Father, how grateful we are for the good news of the gospel. I pray that my grandchild would never cease to be amazed that nothing can separate him "from the love of God that is in Christ Jesus our Lord" (Romans 8:39). Please use this truth, Lord, to promote spiritual health, growth, and maturity. May the heart of my grandchild always be humble and thankful that he is known by such a great and loving God.

Application: Share with your grandchild how excited you were to receive the good news of his birth and the awe you felt that God had blessed your family with such a precious new life.

June 24

"Before his downfall a man's heart is proud, but humility comes before honor."

—Proverbs 18:12

Lord, thank You for reminding us of the natural consequences of a proud heart. As she grows in her faith, please give my grandchild a heart full of humility so that she will not have to experience any downfall caused by pride. Help her to willingly submit to the One who relinquished the honor of heaven and humbled Himself for her sake.

Application: Share the story of Mother Teresa and how she humbly worked with the poor in the streets of Calcutta.

June 25

"Do not wear yourself out to get rich;
have the wisdom to show restraint.
Cast but a glance at riches, and they are
gone, for they will surely sprout wings
and fly off to the sky like an eagle."

—Proverbs 23:4-5

Lord, this verse reminds us that earthly riches are only temporary. Please help my grandchild understand this truth so he will not be tempted to place his faith in wealth, which can disappear. Fill his heart with gratitude for "the unsearchable riches of Christ," which can never be taken away.

Application: Watch a program on birds or eagles, such as one found on www.nationalgeographic.com, and discuss how difficult it is to catch and keep a bird. Share how this proverb says that riches are like the birds—elusive and fleeting.

June 26

"Pride goes before destruction,
a haughty spirit before a fall."

—Proverbs 16:18

Lord, You warn us countless times in Your Word that pride is insidious. Please help my grandchild see how foolish it is to trust in her own wisdom. I pray that she would acknowledge Your wisdom as supreme and willingly submit herself to Your guidance and direction. Thank You, Father, for Your promise to lift her up as she humbles herself before You (see James 4:10).

Application: Teach your grandchild the word *insidious.* Discuss how its meaning—"dangerous, subtle, sinister"—is related to the destructiveness of pride.

June 27

"A heart at peace gives life to the body, but envy rots the bones."

—Proverbs 14:30

Father, it is often tempting to compare ourselves to others. The result of comparison, however, is often pride or envy, and that is not how You call us to live. Thank You for the life of my grandchild. Please develop in him a heart of gratitude for the unique way he was made. Help him to walk humbly with You throughout his days, not being jealous of the gifts or abilities You have given others, but rejoicing in his own.

Application: Talk with your grandchild about what we can do to keep ourselves healthy — eat appropriate foods, exercise, get enough sleep, etc. Explain that we also stay healthy by seeking God because only He can give us the true peace that our bodies, minds, and spirits need.

June 28

"He who mocks the poor shows contempt for their Maker; whoever gloats over disaster will not go unpunished."

—Proverbs 17:5

Lord, we know that all we are and all we have is from Your gracious hand. Please give my grandchild the wisdom to see all people as Jesus saw them—individuals created in Your image. I pray that You would give her a heart of compassion for those who are needy. May she never forget that she, too, has been a needy recipient of much grace and mercy from the Lord Jesus.

Application: Discuss with your grandchild appropriate ways to honor God and to show gratitude for His many blessings in your lives—giving generously through service or donations, helping others, random acts of kindness, etc.

June 29

"Like a bird that strays from its nest
is a man who strays from his home."

—Proverbs 27:8

Lord, there is an old saying: "The grass is always greener on the other side of the fence." I pray that my grandchild would see the folly and danger of a life characterized by discontent and restlessness. Please help him to demonstrate humility with the gifts and blessings You have given him. May he have contentment and true rest as he seeks to be faithful to Your call on his life.

Application: Make a bird's nest out of twigs and discuss how dangerous it would be for a mother bird to desert her baby birds in the nest. Then discuss how grateful your grandchild can be for the care he receives in his home.

June 30

"Haughty eyes and a proud heart,
the lamp of the wicked, are sin."

– Proverbs 21:4

Lord, we acknowledge that You are the Giver of "every good and perfect gift"—of all that we are and all that we have. There is no room, therefore, for any pride in ourselves, our position, or our possessions. Please develop in my grandchild a heart of gratitude for all the gifts she has received from You. I pray, Father, that her path would be illumined by the "light of the world," Jesus Himself (John 8:12), so that she may see clearly to follow You in true humility.

Application: Read the story of "Cinderella" with your grandchild and discover how the pride and arrogance of the stepsisters resulted in Cinderella's poor treatment. Discuss how the outcome of the story might have been different if the stepsisters had been humble instead of haughty.

MAY MY GRANDCHILD LIVE A LIFE OF...

INTEGRITY

JULY

July 1

"The righteous man walks in his integrity;
his children are blessed after him."

—Proverbs 20:7 (NKJV)

Father, we are thankful for the legacy of righteousness left by the generations before us. Please help my grandchild to know that You care about families. I pray that You would impress upon her the importance of leaving a godly inheritance to her children. Allow her to rejoice in the knowledge that her children will be blessed because of her choice to live a life of integrity.

Application: Make a family tree with your grandchild. As you work, talk about her ancestors and those who will come after her.

July 2

"The LORD abhors dishonest scales,
but accurate weights are his delight."

—PROVERBS 11:1

Lord, it is so easy to compromise in today's world—it almost seems to be expected. But I pray that my grandchild would hold himself to a higher standard and weigh his words and actions on Your scales. You delight in those who live honestly, but You have some very strong opinions about those who cheat.

Application: Read John 14:6 with your grandchild. Point out that Jesus calls Himself "the Way, the Truth, and the Life." Encourage your grandchild to ask Jesus to show him the truth in all situations.

July 3

"The Proverbs of Solomon son of David, king of Israel: for attaining wisdom and discipline; for understanding words of insight."

—Proverbs 1:1-2

Lord, I pray that You would give my grandchild the wisdom, discipline, and insight to live a life of integrity—a life that brings honor to You at all times. Help her to know Your Word and to apply its truths to the situations she will face. Allow her to make choices that are consistent with Your will and purpose for her life.

Application: Read 1 Chronicles 4:9-10 with your grandchild. Discuss how Jabez lived an honorable life despite personal pain. Then read how God blessed Jabez by answering his prayers.

July 4

"Do not testify
against your neighbor
without cause, or use your lips
to deceive."

—Proverbs 24:28

Lord, the words we say can be used to encourage or to destroy. They can be used to edify or to criticize. They can be used to reveal truth or to deceive. I pray that my grandchild would be a person of integrity so that the words he speaks would be powerful instruments for You. May he learn at a young age to value absolute truth.

Application: Help your grandchild to say something nice to a neighbor. Suggest that he think of several pleasant greetings or simple chores he can say and do to be a blessing in the neighborhood.

July 5

"Let love and faithfulness never leave you;
bind them around your neck,
write them on the tablet of your heart.
Then you will win favor and a good name
in the sight of God and man."

—Proverbs 3:3-4

Thank You, Lord, for clearly and beautifully declaring in Your Word the choices we need to make in order to live favorably in Your sight. I pray that my grandchild will understand that two of the most desirable virtues are love and faithfulness and that consistently demonstrating these traits pleases You as well as others. Thank You, too, for always keeping Your promises to Your children—You bestow favor and a good name on those who love You and are faithful.

Application: Help your grandchild make a heart necklace, using construction paper and string. Write the words *Love* and *Faithfulness* on the heart to demonstrate the truth of this proverb. Suggest that she wear it as a reminder of God's love and faithfulness to her.

July 6

"The tongue of the wise
commends knowledge,
but the mouth of the fool
gushes folly."

-- Proverbs 15:2

Lord, in Your grace You have given us the right to choose. We can be wise or foolish, knowledgeable or senseless, uplifting or discouraging. Help my grandchild, Lord, to desire wisdom, to display knowledge, and to speak encouragement to others. I pray especially that he would think before he speaks. Help his words and conduct to be reflective of Your hand on his life.

Application: Demonstrate what gushing water looks like by placing your hand at the end of a running hose or under a faucet. Explain that this proverb states that the words of a fool gush like water pouring out in every direction and not being useful.

July 7

"Like a club or a sword or a sharp arrow is the man who gives false testimony against his neighbor."

—Proverbs 25:18

You tell us in this proverb, Lord, that words can be used like weapons. They can be released without much forethought and cause injury, destruction, and even death. Help my grandchild, Lord, to love her neighbors and to speak the truth that brings enlightenment and encouragement to their souls. May her words be used for healing and not for harm, reflecting a life of integrity.

Application: Tell your grandchild how it hurts you when someone tells a lie about you. Ask her how it makes her feel. Discuss the best way to respond to such a situation.

July 8

"Righteousness guards the man of integrity,
but wickedness overthrows the sinner."

– Proverbs 13:6

Lord, thank You for the privilege of being a grandparent. I commit my grandchild into Your hands and ask that You would help him to live a life of integrity. Develop in him first a desire for Your righteousness that will guard his conduct. Then, Lord, please help him to be consistent in his walk with You.

Application: Ask your grandchild whom he wants to be like when he grows up—and why.

July 9

"Better a little with righteousness than much gain with injustice."

—Proverbs 16:8

Father, living a life of integrity means "right" living. I pray that my grandchild would live according to Your principles and precepts, whether she has little material wealth or much. I ask that she would not be tempted to be unjust in her dealings with other people for the purpose of illicit gain. Help her to find contentment in all circumstances.

Application: Talk to your grandchild about the meaning of injustice. Tell how the Bible does not want us to violate the rights of others or to treat them unfairly. Share some examples of injustice on a massive scale, such as the imprisonment and execution of approximately six million Jewish people during World War II.

July 10

"The righteous detest the dishonest;
the wicked detest the upright."

—Proverbs 29:27

Father, this proverb reminds us of the state of man as described throughout the Bible: right vs. wrong, good vs. bad, pure vs. corrupt, moral vs. immoral. Since righteousness and wickedness are opposites, each cannot tolerate the other. I pray that my grandchild would become a man of integrity and that his actions would reflect the strong and honorable character You are developing in him.

Application: Read 1 Samuel 24:1-7 to your grandchild. Discuss this encounter between David and King Saul, when David's righteous character would not permit him to hurt Saul, even though he may have been tempted.

July 11

"He who winks maliciously causes grief,
and a chattering fool comes to ruin."

—Proverbs 10:10

Father, thank You for being concerned about every aspect of my grandchild's life and for giving her words to live by. I pray that she would never secretly plot against anyone or think she could "wink" her way out of mischief. I also ask, Lord, that You would help her to control her speech and to speak wisely rather than foolishly. As she conducts her life with integrity, I pray that You would help her to acknowledge Your hand of blessing.

Application: Practice "winking" at each other. Then discuss how some people use this as a signal that they are scheming against someone else.

July 12

"To do what is right and just
is more acceptable to the LORD
than sacrifice."

— PROVERBS 21:3

Father, sometimes our hearts deceive us into believing that it is easier to ask forgiveness for a wrong committed than to do what is right in the first place. But this proverb tells us that God wants just the opposite! He loves hearts of obedience. Help my grandchild to know Your Word so well that the choice between right and wrong comes easily.

Application: Read Psalm 119:105 together: "Your word is a lamp to my feet and a light for my path" and discuss how God's Word can give us direction and clarity for making decisions that will please Him.

July 13

"Two things I ask of you, O Lord;
do not refuse me before I die:
keep falsehood and lies far from me;
give me neither poverty nor riches,
but give me only my daily bread."

—Proverbs 30:7-8

Lord, I am so grateful that You know the perfect path for my grandchild. I pray that she would both desire to know the truth and to speak the truth. I ask You to give her materially only what You deem best for her—what she needs, not necessarily everything she wants. Bless her, Lord, as she learns to live differently from the principles dictated by this world.

Application: Memorize the Lord's Prayer together (see Matthew 6:9-13). Talk about what it means not to fall into temptation and to trust God to meet our daily needs.

July 14

"If a man pays back evil for good,
evil will never leave his house."

—Proverbs 17:13

Father, I pray that my grandchild would never be tempted to repay good with evil. The cycle of evil can be so destructive that once it starts, it seems never to end. Help my grandchild to learn the principle of treating others as he would like to be treated. Help him to remember that living a life that honors You is the best choice.

Application: With your grandchild, look up the definition of *honor* in a dictionary. Discuss ways to honor God and others.

July 15

"Hatred stirs up dissension,
but love covers over all wrongs."

—Proverbs 10:12

Father, I pray that my grandchild would always be aware of the covering of love that You have placed over her. Please allow her to extend that covering to include others who may be more difficult to love. Let forgiveness, acceptance, mercy, grace and honor be consistently demonstrated in her daily life. Let her view Your love as a canopy that "covers over all wrongs."

Application: Set up a tent together or make a "pretend tent" out of blankets. Discuss how God's love is like a canopy that makes us feel safe and secure.

July 16

"The crucible for silver
and the furnace for gold,
but man is tested
by the praise he receives."

– Proverbs 27:21

Lord, most of the time we don't think of praise as a test, but clearly it is. Help my grandchild to pass this type of exam with flying colors. I pray he would understand that all praise and glory belongs to You…each day he lives is a gift he has been given…each honor he receives is because of Your work in his life. Help him to accept praise with the humble recognition that all we have and all we are come from You.

Application: Help your grandchild to make a list of the talents and abilities God has given him. Then thank Him for them together.

July 17

"A good name is more desirable
than great riches;
to be esteemed
is better than silver or gold."

—PROVERBS 22:1

Lord, our reputations are reflections of the choices we make. I pray that my grandchild will never act in a manner that would compromise her character or shame her name. Help her to see that a good name is more valuable than anything the world can offer. Help her to maintain her reputation by walking with integrity.

Application: Ask your grandchild to tell you about someone she likes and respects. Discuss the character traits that attracted her to that person.

July 18

"A false witness
will not go unpunished,
and he who pours out lies
will not go free."

—Proverbs 19:5

Lord, we can't say that You don't warn Your people of the consequences of their actions! Thank You for pointing out the clear truth that dishonesty will be punished. I pray that my grandchild will speak the truth in love and kindness. I pray that his words may be glorifying to You, edifying to others, and reflective of Your Spirit in him. I also pray that he may feel the freedom that comes with that kind of lifestyle.

Application: Read John 8:31-32 with your grandchild. Discuss how the teachings of Jesus set us free.

July 19

"The man of integrity walks securely,
but he who takes crooked paths
will be found out."

—PROVERBS 10:9

*Lord, thank You for directing my grandchild's path.
I ask also, Lord, that You develop in her the quality of integrity—honesty and truthfulness, without compromise.
Help her avoid "crooked paths"—even the description suggests twisted and distorted living.
Please keep her on the straight and narrow path,
walking under Your protection.*

Application: Take a walk together and talk about the different routes you might take to reach your destination. Discuss why some choices are better than others and how we should always make the best choices possible.

July 20

"The integrity of the upright guides them,
but the unfaithful are destroyed
by their duplicity."

—Proverbs 11:3

Lord, today I pray specifically that my grandchild will become a man of integrity. Your Word assures us that upright living will guide, preserve, and protect him. I ask, Father, that You would help him to be uncompromising in his walk with You and that he would never have to suffer the consequences of unfaithfulness.

Application: Discuss how God used a pillar of cloud during the day and a pillar of fire at night to guide the Israelites in the wilderness (see Exodus 13:21-22). Explain that He continues to lead us today by His Word and His Spirit.

July 21

"When a man's ways
are pleasing to the LORD,
he makes even his enemies
live at peace with him."

—PROVERBS 16:7

Lord, thank You for this wonderful assurance that when our actions are pleasing to You, the result will be peace with others. Throughout history, man has tried unsuccessfully to achieve peace, yet Your Word gives us a clear directive on how to accomplish that goal. I pray that my grandchild's ways would be pleasing to You and that You would bless her relationships with others.

Application: Read Isaiah 11:6 to your grandchild: "The wolf will live with the lamb, the leopard will lie down with the goat, the calf and the lion and the yearling together; and a little child will lead them." Discuss how this prophecy about God's future reign tells us that all creation will live together in peace and harmony.

July 22

"Food gained by fraud
tastes sweet to a man,
but he ends up
with a mouth full of gravel."

—Proverbs 20:17

Lord, this proverb illustrates the fact that we don't always know what is best for us. We may desire something, no matter the cost, and then find out it wasn't worth the price. Help my grandchild to have an upright and honorable character, to hide Your Word in his heart, and to know right from wrong.

Application: Discuss with your grandchild what a mouthful of gravel or dirt would taste like. Would it be delicious? Nutritious? Explain how this verse says that when we cheat, the results are like eating dirt—very unpleasant.

July 23

"The tongue of the righteous
is choice silver;
but the heart of the wicked
is of little value."

—Proverbs 10:20

Father, You tell us that our mouths speak what flows from our hearts. Please draw my grandchild so close to You that her words would reflect the work that You are doing in her. Help her to understand that she will be accountable for everything she says and that her words have eternal significance (see Matthew 12:36-37).

Application: Wash some pieces of silverware with your grandchild and discuss how valuable they are. Stress the fact that our words are even more valuable.

July 24

"A false witness will perish,
and whoever listens to him
will be destroyed forever."

—Proverbs 21:28

Lord, the message in this verse is quite blunt and emphasizes the importance of being able to differentiate the truth from a lie. Please, Lord, give my grandchild the desire to know You so well that he will be able to discern an honest person from a liar. Help him to align himself with people of integrity who speak the truth and follow You. Impress on his heart the true hope of eternal life that comes from knowing You as his personal Savior.

Application: Read and discuss 1 Corinthians 15:33: "Do not be misled: 'Bad company corrupts good character.'"

July 25

"The LORD detests men of perverse heart
but he delights in those
whose ways are blameless."

—PROVERBS 11:20

Lord, how easy it is to slip into waywardness—a lifestyle that compromises our convictions and character. I pray that my grandchild would be focused on seeking You. Help her to live honestly and with integrity. Thank You for delighting in Your children who are committed to You.

Application: Talk about the fact that God is pleased when we are truthful and demonstrate integrity.

July 26

"He who winks with his eye
is plotting perversity;
he who purses his lips
is bent on evil."

—Proverbs 16:30

Father, simple, unconscious mannerisms often reveal our true nature. I pray that my grandchild would never pick up the careless speech and crude gestures that the world calls "cool." Instead, may he pursue a life of goodness and integrity reflected by a warm twinkle in his eye and a kind smile.

Application: Tell your grandchild that the way we communicate with others is much more than words. Communication is also accomplished through body language. Practice "winking" and "pursing your lips" when you talk and see how that changes what is being communicated.

July 27

"There is deceit in the hearts
of those who plot evil,
but joy for those
who promote peace."

—Proverbs 12:20

Lord, please help my grandchild to understand that true peace comes from a relationship with You and that it cannot be found through any other means. Give her a heart that is passionate for You. Help her to promote the peace that only You can give by sharing her faith in words and actions. Then let her experience the joy promised to those whose lives consistently honor You.

Application: Read together John 14:27: "Peace I leave with you; my peace I give you. I do not give to you as the world gives. Do not let your hearts be troubled and do not be afraid." Make sure your grandchild understands that it is Jesus Himself who promises to give her supernatural peace. She doesn't ever have to be afraid again!

July 28

"The LORD detests
the thoughts of the wicked,
but those of the pure
are pleasing to him."

—PROVERBS 15:26

Lord, I pray that my grandchild's character would be pure. Help him to center his thoughts on You and Your majesty. Please keep him uncorrupted by the world and its values; instead, allow him to live a life fully dedicated to You. May those around him recognize in him an uncompromising and unwavering walk of faith.

Application: Draw a line with chalk on the sidewalk, or place a strip of tape on the floor. Challenge your grandchild to practice walking on the straight line. Discuss how it takes focus to walk on the line just as it takes focus on God to walk out a life of faith.

July 29

"Honest scales and balances
are from the Lord;
all the weights in the bag
are of his making."

—Proverbs 16:11

Father, this proverb is a reminder that You are concerned about behavior and character and provide many opportunities for Your children to act honestly and uprightly. I pray that my grandchild would recognize Your guidance in her life and that she would choose to live a balanced life. Help her, Lord, when faced with choices, to remember that she should be true to her beliefs.

Application: Talk with your grandchild about what to do when she has done something wrong. Discuss the concepts of confession, repentance, forgiveness, and restoration. If appropriate, share about a time you realized you had done something wrong and how you handled it.

July 30

"With his mouth
the godless destroys his neighbor,
but through knowledge
the righteous escape."

—Proverbs 11:9

Lord, this proverb reminds us that the words we speak can be either destructive or redeeming. I pray, Lord, that my grandchild would make his words pleasing in Your sight and edifying to the community around him. Help him to build up and not destroy others by what he says. Let his speech and his life be consistent with the knowledge You have given him.

Application: Help your grandchild make a list of encouraging words and phrases to say to one another.

July 31

"An evil man is trapped by his sinful talk,
but a righteous man escapes trouble."

—Proverbs 12:13

It is apparent from this proverb that the words we speak can either trap us or help us escape trouble. Father, I pray that my grandchild will be a righteous woman, redeemed through Jesus—one who does not use "sinful talk." Remind her of Your promise to provide an escape for any temptation that comes her way (see 1 Corinthians 10:13). Help her to speak in a manner that will yield blessings to others and will demonstrate her integrity and commitment to You.

Application: Trap a bug in a jar and discuss with your grandchild how, when we're trapped, we are caught in circumstances we don't like. Share what this proverb says about "sinful talk" being a trap that puts us in a place where we don't want to be.

MAY MY GRANDCHILD DEVELOP...

Self-control

AUGUST

August 1

"There is one who speaks
like the piercing of a sword,
but the tongue of the wise
promotes health."

—Proverbs 12:18 (NKJV)

Lord, what a descriptive picture of the injury our words can inflict on others! A sword is sharp, pointed, and can cause great pain. We are also told, however, that words can be like medicine, promoting good health. I pray that my grandchild would understand the power of his tongue and use it carefully and thoughtfully. Please bless his efforts, Father, as he attempts to be an agent of peace and healing.

Application: Make a sword together out of cardboard. Talk about the damage that a sword can do and how it is designed to pierce. Discuss how this proverb tells us that careless words can hurt like a sharp blade, but kind words bring healing.

August 2

"The highway of the upright avoids evil;
he who guards his way guards his life."

—PROVERBS 16:17

Lord, as we walk through this life, it is easy to be sidetracked by the glitter and allure of the world. I pray that my grandchild would have the self-control to take the high road. Please guard her footsteps so that she may avoid stumbling into sin. Thank You that she can depend on Your Spirit to guide and direct her as she faces difficult circumstances.

Application: Read an age-appropriate version (or watch the DVD) of *Pilgrim's Progress*. Discuss how Christian continually had to make the choice to stay on the right path on his journey to the Celestial City.

August 3

"A man of perverse heart
does not prosper;
he whose tongue is deceitful
falls into trouble."

—Proverbs 17:20

Father, help my grandchild to understand that his words should reflect a heart of thoughtfulness and self-control. Keep trouble far from him as he seeks only Your truth. May his mind be so permeated with Jesus' love that everything he says will refresh and strengthen others. Please bless him with a pure heart so that his faith prospers.

Application: Memorize Colossians 3:9a: "Do not lie to each other."

August 4

"The discretion of a man
makes him slow to anger,
and his glory is to
overlook a transgression."

—PROVERBS 19:11 (NKJV)

Father, the life of Jesus exhibits perfect discretion. Based upon Your promise to develop in us a Christ-like character, I ask You to give my grandchild a mind and heart of godly discretion. Please help her to be thoughtful and prudent in all that she does, not quick to respond in anger. May the security of her relationship with You enable her not only to overlook, but to forgive, any transgression aimed her way.

Application: Teach your grandchild some effective ways to manage anger. For example, count to 10 before responding. Other examples: Walk away, or take a deep breath. All these actions allow your grandchild to regain control of her emotions.

August 5

"He who guards his mouth and his tongue keeps himself from calamity."

– Proverbs 21:23

Father, we are grateful for this principle to live by—that if we are careful what we say, we can spare ourselves calamity—"a state of deep distress or misery caused by major misfortune or loss." I ask You, Lord, to give my grandchild the ability to apply this principle. Help him to think before he speaks. May he guard his tongue—before he says something he will later regret!

Application: Share with your grandchild the saying: "Don't put your foot in your mouth!" Although this is a humorous picture, it means that someone has spoken without thinking, resulting in an awkward or impossible predicament.

August 6

"Whoever flatters his neighbor
is spreading a net for his feet."

– Proverbs 29:5

Father, You know we sometimes hide behind a mask of flattering words and do not speak truthfully. Please protect my grandchild from such hypocrisy. Help her to control her conversation so that she is not trapped in lies and deceit. In all circumstances help her to be genuine and authentic so that her neighbors will know her to be a trustworthy friend.

Application: Take your grandchild to a play. Discuss how the actors and actresses are only pretending and that a play is not necessarily reflective of true life. Share how we need to be honest in our real relationships with others.

August 7

"Even a fool is thought wise
if he keeps silent,
and discerning
if he holds his tongue."

—Proverbs 17:28

Father, we are grateful for the gift of language. We know, however, that sometimes the words that are spoken can reveal the world's foolishness as well as Your wisdom. Please help my grandchild to use self-control in expressing his thoughts, possibly choosing to remain silent. I pray that he would be swift to hear and slow to speak in order to reflect Your love.

Application: As a method of reinforcing the principle of being discerning and self- controlled, help your grandchild draw or find the illustration of the three monkeys: one covers his eyes, one covers his mouth, and one covers his ears. Then quote the old adage together: "See no evil, speak no evil, hear no evil."

August 8

"A quick-tempered man
acts foolishly,
and a man of wicked intentions
is hated."

—Proverbs 14:17 (NKJV)

Father, thank You for the variety of unique personalities and dispositions You have created. I pray that my grandchild would have an awareness of her temperament and not give vent to unchecked emotions. Please give her the wisdom to see that tantrums or angry outbursts rarely represent the righteousness of God. May she experience Your power to quench the fire of inappropriate anger in her heart as soon as it occurs.

Application: Light a candle with your grandchild and then demonstrate how to put out the flame by carefully dousing it with water. Talk about how we also sometimes need to quench anger in our own hearts. We can do this by asking God to show us when our anger is appropriate and when it is wrong.

August 9

"The tongue has the power of life and death, and those who love it will eat its fruit."

— Proverbs 18:21

Lord, You have told us that we are "fearfully and wonderfully made" (Psalm. 139:14). While it is difficult to grasp that something as small as our tongue could hold tremendous power, this proverb says it is true. I pray that my grandchild would come to understand the impact of his words. Please give him the self-control to speak "life" and not "death" to others.

<u>Application:</u> Make a list of some words and phrases that would encourage and bring life to your grandchild. Use one each day for the rest of the month. Suggest that he do the same and practice using his new love language with his siblings and friends.

August 10

"A patient man has great understanding, but a quick-tempered man displays folly."

—Proverbs 14:29

Father, please give my grandchild the ability to control her impatience. Allow her to understand that You are sovereign in all situations and that You direct her comings and goings. Teach her not to expect to have her way in all things. Please show her that Your love desires the best for her; then help her to wait patiently on Your timing.

Application: Work a puzzle with your grandchild. Discuss how patient one has to be to find the right pieces when putting a puzzle together. The same is true with God's work.

August 11

"Do you see a man who speaks in haste?
There is more hope for a fool than for him."

— Proverbs 29:20

Father, we live in an age of great speed. We want everything done quickly. Certainly this is true when it comes to our conversation. Please help my grandchild to value patience and really listen before making a comment when someone is talking. Help him to see the dangers of impulsive speech and give him wisdom in his responses.

Application: Enjoy a story time with your grandchild in which you share experiences from your childhood when things took a lot longer than they do today—travel, cooking, mail, etc. Ask your grandchild if there are any areas of his life in which he needs more patience and self-control.

August 12

"A perverse man stirs up dissension,
and a gossip separates close friends."

—Proverbs 16:28

Lord, this proverb reveals characteristics that I certainly do not want to surface in my grandchild—troublemaking, perversity, and gossip. Instead, please help her to have an agreeable spirit, to be pure and wise when she speaks, and to have the self-control to respond appropriately in all situations. Let her know that her words, rightly spoken, have the power to unite and bring people together.

Application: Read Jesus' prayer for His disciples in John 17:23 with your grandchild: "May they be brought to complete unity to let the world know that you sent me." Discuss the fact that Jesus does not want anything to separate Christians and that we need to guard our speech so that it does not destroy friendships.

August 13

"A wise man fears the LORD
and shuns evil,
but a fool is hotheaded
and reckless."

—PROVERBS 14:16

Lord, we can certainly act foolishly at any age by behaving carelessly and without thought. However, we demonstrate wisdom when we exhibit restraint. I pray that my grandchild would find delight in demonstrating this type of self-control. Please strengthen his desire to live a life that is honoring to You.

Application: Act out the story in Daniel 6 of the time Daniel shunned evil by refusing to pray to anyone but the true and living God. Talk about how God protected him in the lion's den because of his faithfulness.

August 14

"If you have played the fool
and exalted yourself,
or if you have planned evil,
clap your hand over your mouth!"

—Proverbs 30:32

Lord, help my grandchild to know when she has been foolish. Please allow her to control her behavior and words so that they would not be self-promoting, but instead would glorify You. May Your Spirit make this proverb come alive for my grandchild and show her how to avoid bragging or plotting some evil scheme with her companions. I do pray that my grandchild would find an effective manner of practicing self-control.

Application: Make a game out of the practice of putting your hand over your mouth when tempted to say something hurtful, insulting, or boastful. Record how many times during the day you have to stop yourself from speaking. The one with the highest count provides a treat for the other!

August 15

"The words of a gossip
are like choice morsels;
they go down to a man's inmost parts."

—Proverbs 18:8

Father, please help my grandchild understand that even though gossip may seem like a "juicy" morsel—intriguing to hear and to pass along—it is generally destructive. I pray that You would teach him self-control and give him the ability to resist idle talk or rumor. Instead, may he study the words of Jesus and speak only what is true, noble, and substantive.

<u>Application:</u> Enjoy a healthy treat with your grandchild and discuss how, like "choice morsels" nourish our bodies, truthful words nourish our souls.

August 16

"Better is a dry crust with peace and quiet, than a house full of feasting, with strife."

– Proverbs 17:1

Lord, please enable my grandchild to see that wealth, power, and prestige will not bring quiet and rest to her home. This proverb assures us that it is better to have just a little with peace than an abundance in the midst of chaos. I pray that my grandchild would learn to control her appetite for worldly possessions. Let her realize that it is only Jesus, the Bread of Life, who will truly satisfy her heart hunger and bring harmony to her dwelling place.

Application: Bake bread or rolls with your grandchild. Discuss how bread can remind us of Jesus—our Provider and our Provision. Mention how satisfying the basic necessities of life can be when enjoyed in a peaceful atmosphere.

August 17

"From the fruit of his lips
a man enjoys good things,
but the unfaithful
have a craving for violence."

—Proverbs 13:2

Father, this proverb says that the words we speak can bring us good things. I pray that my grandchild will "crave" only those things that delight You and draw him closer to You, Lord. I pray that the "fruit of his lips" would represent the fruit of Your Spirit in his life—"love, joy, peace, patience, kindness, goodness, faithfulness, gentleness, and self-control" (Galatians 5:22).

<u>Application:</u> Share some fruit as a snack. Talk with your grandchild about the "fruit" of his speech and how he can demonstrate the fruit of God's Spirit in his life with every word he speaks.

August 18

"Do not boast about tomorrow,
for you do not know
what a day may bring forth."

—Proverbs 27:1

Lord, while it is true that we do not know what tomorrow may bring, we do know that You hold all our tomorrows in Your sovereign hand. Please give my grandchild the self-control not to boast about her possessions, her power, or her influence or to think that she alone can order her future. Let her boast only in You as she trusts in Your love and guidance.

Application: Read the story of Noah to your grandchild (see Genesis 6-8). Let her know how God directed Noah's path in a very unexpected way. Even when everyone was laughing at him, Noah listened to God and obeyed, carrying out what seemed to be an outrageous idea!

August 19

"He who goes about as a talebearer
reveals secrets;
therefore do not associate
with one who flatters with his lips."

— Proverbs 20:19 (NKJV)

Father, Jesus knew the heart and was never fooled by outward appearances or flattery. Please give my grandchild the desire to be a sincere and trustworthy friend and the discernment to choose as his friends, people with these same characteristics. Bless him with relationships that are built on honesty and authenticity, and use these relationships to help him develop good judgment and self-control.

Application: Discuss with your grandchild what it means to be a friend. Read the story of David and Jonathan (1 Samuel 18-20) and discuss how God used their friendship to build strong character.

August 20

"Do not say,
'I'll pay you back for this wrong!'
Wait for the LORD,
and he will deliver you."

—PROVERBS 20:22

Lord, You are the only perfect Judge, who knows everything about everyone and every situation. Please help my grandchild understand that she must never seek to repay evil with evil, but instead must trust in You to work things out. Allow her to receive Your grace so she can then pass it on to the wrongdoer by controlling her responses, loving her enemy, and waiting patiently for You.

Application: Share a personal story about a time when someone hurt you. Describe how you felt and what you did. Be honest as you share. Tell your grandchild how you might react if you could do it over again.

August 21

"He who covers over an offense
promotes love,
but whoever repeats the matter
separates close friends."

—Proverbs 17:9

Father, please enable my grandchild to know the value of relationships and to seek to preserve them. There will be times when he is tempted to gossip or share embarrassing stories, but I pray that You would give him restraint. Help him to demonstrate Your love by controlling the information he shares. Enable him to understand that love is not primarily an emotional feeling, but a proactive work, showing compassion for someone.

Application: Play a game with your grandchild where you are not allowed to speak, but must do something to show kindness to another person. You could put a scarf over your mouth as a reminder not to speak. When you have decided on an action, take turns showing compassion without using words.

August 22

"If you find honey, eat just enough—too much of it, and you will vomit."

—Proverbs 25:16

Father, thank You for my grandchild and all the blessings You have lavished on us. I pray that she would have a thankful heart and acknowledge You as the Giver of all good things. Help her to be wise in the use of Your many blessings and to know how to practice restraint. Please give her the self-control to eat only what is good for her and to be content with what she has.

Application: Read some of the stories of *Winnie the Pooh* to your grandchild. Discover together how Winnie's gluttonous love of honey often gets him into trouble.

August 23

"If a man loudly blesses his neighbor
early in the morning,
it will be taken as a curse."

—Proverbs 27:14

Lord, we know that we often act hastily without thinking things through. This proverb reminds us that even a kindness extended in the wrong manner can be perceived as an insult. I pray that my grandchild will be sensitive, tactful, and discerning as he lives in relationship with others.

Application: Ask your grandchild how he likes to spend his mornings. Is he an outgoing young person who likes interaction, or does he prefer quiet space for reflection? Share how we should be considerate and respectful of the needs of others.

August 24

"He who guards his lips guards his life,
but he who speaks rashly will come to ruin."

—Proverbs 13:3

Lord, thank You for the ability to communicate and express our thoughts. Please help my grandchild think carefully before she speaks, weighing the impact her words will have on herself and others. May she seek to speak only words of truth and substance. I pray, Father, that her wisely chosen words would reflect a heartfelt desire to honor You.

Application: Ask your grandchild if she has ever seen a mouth guard such as those used for soccer, hockey, football, etc. Describe how a mouth guard is used to protect the teeth. Share that in this proverb, God tells us to guard our mouths—by being careful what we say.

August 25

"A fool finds no pleasure in understanding but delights in airing his own opinions."

—Proverbs 18:2

Lord, acting and speaking foolishly brings such disgrace to an individual. I pray that my grandchild would have the self-control to choose Your ways and words. Give him the desire to learn and to understand what he has learned. May he not rush to express his opinions and views but take greater delight in hearing Your voice than in hearing the sound of his own.

Application: Take your grandchild to a local pet store. Observe a parrot, who only mimics what he hears and has no understanding of the words. Share with your grandchild the truth that God wants us to use self-control and wisdom when we speak.

August 26

"A gentle answer turns away wrath,
but a harsh word stirs up anger."

—Proverbs 15:1

Father, it is obvious from this proverb that words have the power to elicit certain responses for good or evil. Please help my grandchild to choose words that please You. May her mind be so aligned with the mind of Christ that her words mirror Jesus' love. Give her the self-control to express gentleness regardless of the circumstances.

Application: Suggest that your grandchild look into a mirror and see how it reflects her image. Share how God wants us to reflect His image in all that we say and do.

August 27

"Like a city whose walls are broken down
is a man who lacks self-control."

—Proverbs 25:28

Lord, walls have played an important role in providing protection for cities throughout history. I ask that my grandchild would also understand the importance of a wall of self-control in his own life. Please help him to guard his attitude, words, and behavior so that they would be pleasing to You. May You use this kind of discipline to continue to conform his character to Your image.

Application: Take a walk with your grandchild and observe the different kinds of walls and fences. How are they used? To shelter? To protect? To keep out intruders? Discuss how walls also serve as boundaries and how God gives us self-control to maintain the boundaries in our own lives.

August 28

"Do not slander a servant to his master, or he will curse you, and you will pay for it."

—Proverbs 30:10

Father, thank You for another reminder to control what we say and how we say it. We need to be truthful and to edify one another. I pray that my grandchild would not be tempted to insult others or to interfere in their activities. Instead, please give her a discerning spirit and a compassionate heart and allow her actions to reflect her trust in You.

Application: Discuss with your grandchild the consequences of interfering in a fight between two dogs. Isn't this similar to what might happen if you got in the middle of a misunderstanding between two people? Although it may be tempting to get involved, there could be serious repercussions—and you might "pay for it"!

August 29

"An angry man stirs up dissension,
and a hot-tempered one
commits many sins."

—Proverbs 29:22

Lord, You have created human beings with a wide range of emotions. One of these emotions, anger, can cause great destruction when uncontrolled. Would You help my grandchild, Father, see the similarity between unbridled anger and a forest fire? Please give him the understanding that anger can damage relationships just as a forest fire damages the landscape. Help him to control his responses and to replace any inappropriate anger with Your love.

Application: Find pictures of forest fires and discuss with your grandchild how difficult they are to control. Relate these fires to the emotion of anger: Once loosed, a few spiteful words, like sparks, can start a blaze that can quickly rage out of control and ruin a wonderful friendship.

August 30

"Starting a quarrel is like breaching a dam;
so drop the matter
before a dispute breaks out."

—PROVERBS 17:14

Father, this proverb is such an accurate reflection of life: once a quarrel has started, it is like a dam breaking, with the hurtful words spilling out in a flood. I pray that my grandchild would exercise self-control when she finds herself in contentious situations. Allow her to be an agent of grace by demonstrating Your love and kindness and thus peaceably resolving any disagreement.

Application: Read the story "The Little Dutch Boy" to your grandchild. The boy's quick action stopped a dam from breaking. Similarly, our quick action and control of our tongues can stop arguments before they begin.

August 31

"Better a patient man than a warrior,
a man who controls his temper
than one who takes a city."

—Proverbs 16:32

Father, this proverb tells us that there is great power and strength in controlling our emotions. Please fill my grandchild with Your presence so that he may exhibit self-control and govern his feelings wisely. May he learn that You are more pleased with a person who controls his temper than with a warrior who subdues an entire city!

Application: Read to your grandchild the Bible story about Esau and how he sold his birthright for a bowl of stew (see Genesis 25:29-33). By not demonstrating self-control, Esau forfeited something he wanted very much.

MAY MY GRANDCHILD CULTIVATE...

STEWARDSHIP

SEPTEMBER

September 1

"He who gathers crops in summer
is a wise son,
but he who sleeps during harvest
is a disgraceful son."

– Proverbs 10:5

Lord, I pray that my grandchild would be a good steward of her time. Help her to use it wisely—to know when to work, when to sleep, and when to play. Allow her to honor, and not disgrace, her family as she properly balances work and rest. Thank You that You have provided the day for labor and the night for refreshment. Please help my grandchild use her time to Your glory.

Application: Find a "pick-your-own" orchard or garden at harvest time—apples, blueberries, strawberries—and plan a day to gather the produce with your grandchild. As you pick the fruits or vegetables, discuss how the Lord has ordained the seasons for specific reasons and expects us to be good stewards of the resources, time, and opportunities He gives us.

September 2

"In his heart a man plans his course, but the Lord determines his steps."

—Proverbs 16:9

O Lord, we praise You and acknowledge that You are the sovereign God over all the universe. I pray that my grandchild would align his heart and desires with Your Word and will. Help him to trust You to guide him in each decision he makes. Thank You for the assurance that as he releases his plans to You, he can have the confidence that You will show him the next step to take.

Application: Share with your grandchild the story of the magician Balaam's encounter with the angel of the Lord in Numbers 22. God allowed a *donkey* to speak for Him—and change Balaam's wicked plans! Point out how God can use anything and anyone to accomplish His purposes.

September 3

"She considers a field
and buys it;
out of her earnings
she plants a vineyard."

—Proverbs 31:16

Lord, thank You for this example of careful consideration and forethought. The woman in this proverb invested well and reaped the rewards of that action. I pray the same for my grandchild. Help her to have discernment about how best to use her resources. Bless her with the understanding that because all she has comes from You, it should be used for Your glory and You will reward her efforts.

Application: Read a biography to your grandchild or tell about a man or woman who used his/her God-given gifts for an extraordinary accomplishment. Suggestions for individuals would be: Thomas Edison, Madame Curie, Booker T. Washington, or Susan B. Anthony.

September 4

"He who works his land
will have abundant food,
but he who chases fantasies
lacks judgment."

—Proverbs 12:11

Lord, this proverb describes the results of cultivating the gifts You have given us. Help my grandchild to be a good steward of all the blessings You have bestowed upon him. Allow him to be industrious in his work and not to be distracted by frivolous daydreams. Give him the desire to be productive with the opportunities he has and to honor You with his actions.

Application: Plant a pot of cherry tomatoes and have your grandchild "tend" the garden—watering, fertilizing, placing it in the sunlight, etc. Share how this attentive care is one way that he can be a good steward of the gifts God has given him.

September 5

"She watches over the affairs
of her household
and does not eat the bread of idleness."

—Proverbs 31:27

Father, help my grandchild to achieve a healthy balance of work and rest. Please keep her from a pattern of idleness that would negatively impact her whole family. I ask, Lord, that You would give her an industrious spirit. Help her to learn how to guard her resources so that in the future she will manage her household well.

Application: Find a local park with a balance beam and have your grandchild attempt to walk on the beam. Discuss how life is like this balance beam and we must learn to keep our lives in balance—physically, mentally, and spiritually.

September 6

"The sluggard buries his hand in the dish;
he will not even bring it back to his mouth!"

—Proverbs 19:24

Lord, this verse gives a humorous picture of one who will not enjoy Your provisions because he is too lazy to feed himself. Please help my grandchild to be thankful for all You provide and to understand his responsibility to practice good stewardship. Never let him take for granted the meal on his table and always have him give thanks to You for Your blessings.

Application: Teach your grandchild a blessing to be said or sung before a meal, thanking God for His provisions and asking Him to help us to be good stewards.

September 7

"She is like the merchant ships,
bringing her food from afar.
She gets up while it is still dark;
She provides food for her family
and portions for her servant girls."

—Proverbs 31:14-15

Lord, I pray that my grandchild might be like the woman pictured in Proverbs 31—resourceful, hardworking, diligent, and caring. I ask, Lord, that You would reveal to her how best to live her life in every area. Give her joy in providing a godly example for others.

Application: With your grandchild, study a map of the world. Discuss how each part of the earth can provide different items or goods for our enjoyment. God has given us so much variety and asks us to take good care of the resources He has given us.

September 8

"A righteous man
cares for the needs of his animal,
but the kindest acts
of the wicked are cruel."

—Proverbs 12:10

Father, You are the Creator of all living things, so You love animals too! Please help my grandchild understand the importance of Your creatures, along with his responsibility to care for the pets You entrust to him. May he always treat Your earthly kingdom with respect, knowing that he is fulfilling Your mandate to be a good steward over Your creation.

Application: Tell your grandchild about any pets or animals you had as a child, and how you took care of them.

September 9

"Dishonest money dwindles away,
but he who gathers money
little by little makes it grow."

—Proverbs 13:11

Lord, I pray that my grandchild would learn to manage her money well. Help her to use her finances wisely and to be diligent in saving. Teach her to be a good steward of all that You give her—whether it be material or spiritual blessings. Allow her to experience bountiful results of good stewardship in both faith and finances and to give You the glory for it all.

Application: With your grandchild, make a piggy bank out of a jar or plastic bottle. Regularly put change in the little bank and watch the amount of money grow!

September 10

"Commit to the LORD
whatever you do,
and your plans will succeed."

—PROVERBS 16:3

Lord, this proverb tells us that we need to place our plans in Your hands in order to be successful. I pray that my grandchild would be deliberate in seeking You to direct his paths. Help him to be a good steward of his time and talents as he trusts You for the results. I am so grateful that You know what is best for him.

Application: Memorize Romans 8:28 together: "And we know that in all things God works for the good of those who love him, who have been called according to his purpose." Share the meaning of this verse: Even when our plans do not work out the way we think they should, God will bring good in "all things."

September 11

"When it snows, she has no fear
for her household;
for all of them are clothed in scarlet."

—PROVERBS 31:21

Lord, thank You that we do not ever have to fear the unknown; You are our guardian and protector at all times. Yet, Father, we know that both spiritual and physical preparations are necessary for the troublesome times in our lives. I pray that my grandchild will carefully guard her resources so that she would be prepared when difficulty comes. Please help her to dig a deep well of faith and love from which she can draw spiritual strength to enable her to face the hard times.

Application: With your grandchild, put together a kit for emergency preparedness. In a box, place a Bible, flashlight, battery-operated radio, medical supplies, etc. Most importantly, remind her that she needs to be prepared for emergencies by knowing and living out God's Word.

September 12

"A simple man believes anything,
but a prudent man
gives thought to his steps."

—Proverbs 14:15

Lord, this verse reminds us that we should give careful deliberation to the plans we make; it is not wise to make rash decisions or react without thought. Nor is it wise to be careless with the time and opportunities You give us. Please help my grandchild to be conscientious in his planning. Above all, please help him to seek You and Your direction before moving forward on any decision.

Application: Plan a trip with your grandchild. Look at a map together and talk about the best route to reach your destination (roads, highways, means of transportation, etc.). Share that when we plan a trip, we consult a map. But when planning our lives, the Bible is our best guide.

September 13

"She sees that her trading is profitable,
and her lamp does not go out at night.
In her hand she holds the distaff
and grasps the spindle with her fingers."

—Proverbs 31:18-19

Father, thank You for this portrait of an ambitious, knowledgeable, and talented person. We are all made in Your image, and so I know You have also designed my grandchild with special talents and abilities. Allow her to be creative and energetic in their use. Help her to rejoice in her own design and develop her gifts wisely.

Application: Help your grandchild draw a self-portrait. Reaffirm her special talents and abilities as you complete this project. Ask her how she can use her gifts for God.

September 14

"Of what use is money in the hand of a fool, since he has no desire to get wisdom?"

– Proverbs 17:16

Lord, you have entrusted us with many gifts and expect us to use them well. The man in this proverb has his priorities backwards. What he really wants is material wealth, not spiritual wealth. I pray that my grandchild would take this warning seriously and desire You before all else. Please help him to allow You to give him what is best for him—righteousness and wisdom—knowing that anything else he really needs will be added.

Application: With your grandchild, make a list of the things that cannot be bought with money—health, wisdom, love, joy, peace, etc. Help him to realize that these are the most valuable possessions of all.

September 15

"A good man leaves an inheritance
for his children's children,
but a sinner's wealth is stored up
for the righteous."

—Proverbs 13:22

Lord, I pray that my grandchild would come to understand that an inheritance is more than earthly wealth. I ask that You give her the passion to accumulate wealth that comes in intangible forms. Help her to be a good steward of all that You give her, but please allow her to see that the most important legacy she can receive or leave behind is spiritual. Thank You for providing an eternal inheritance that is born out of faithfulness and obedience to You.

Application: Discuss with your grandchild the many different types of inheritances we can receive—money, possessions, a good name, godly character, etc. Talk about how we are called to be good stewards of whatever we inherit.

September 16

"The rich rule over the poor,
and the borrower is servant to the lender."

—Proverbs 22:7

Father, thank You that Your Word teaches us about all aspects of life—even our finances. I pray that my grandchild would learn about being a good steward of all that he has, including his money, at an early age. Help him to develop a financial philosophy that is in line with the priorities of Scripture.

Application: Read and then act out the story of the parable of the talents from Matthew 25:14-28 with your grandchild. Explain that this Scripture points out how the Lord entrusts us with many types of gifts, and we need to be good stewards of everything He gives us.

September 17

"Ants are creatures of little strength,
yet they store up their food in the summer."

—Proverbs 30:25

Father, what great lessons in stewardship are taught by ants. Though small and weak, they are able, by sheer determination and diligence, to provide for their future. I pray that my grandchild would learn this lesson well: Although she is still a child, she can accomplish what God gives children to do—learn, grow, obey, etc.—foundational truths that can be used in the years to come.

Application: Go to a grocery store or farmer's market and buy an abundance of fresh produce. With your grandchild, freeze or can this produce and then store for future use.

September 18

"Many are the plans in a man's heart,
but it is the LORD's purpose that prevails."

—PROVERBS 19:21

Father, it is exciting to consider all the ways in which we can serve You in this life. Yet so often our plans are self-serving instead of God-serving. Please help my grandchild to "dream big," yet surrender those dreams to You. Help him to carefully tend the talents, abilities, and dreams You have given him and to be willing to yield all of them to Your greater purpose.

Application: Memorize with your grandchild Psalm 33:11: "But the plans of the LORD stand firm forever, the purposes of his heart through all generations."

September 19

"She sets about her work vigorously;
her arms are strong for her tasks."

–Proverbs 31:17

Lord, there are times when we forget that being a good steward involves taking care of our physical bodies. I pray that my grandchild would be healthy and strong. Help her to enjoy physical exercise, recreational activity, and Your beautiful outdoors. Please teach her to watch over and care for her entire being—body, soul, and spirit.

Application: Go outside and play a game of catch with your grandchild. Emphasize that while this activity is fun and enjoyable, it is also one way to be a good steward of our bodies.

September 20

"Wine is a mocker and beer a brawler;
whoever is led astray by them is not wise."

—Proverbs 20:1

Lord, temptations to distract us from the focus of our faith seem so inviting. Overindulgence in beer and wine is merely an example of those enticements, and grandchildren are not immune. Materialism, success, education, and prestige can also easily become idols. I ask, Lord, that my grandchild would stand strong in his convictions and dedication to You.

Application: Have an age-appropriate discussion with your grandchild about the wise use of God's provisions. For example, food and drink are necessary for life, but overindulgence will be detrimental to his well-being.

September 21

Gwendolyn June Sagen born

"He who works his land
will have abundant food,
but the one who chases fantasies
will have his fill of poverty."

—Proverbs 28:19

Thank You, Lord, for the many unique ways in which You equip Your people. Help my grandchild to seek Your direction and to be faithful in the work that You have called her to do. Allow her the privilege of fulfilling her calling rather than chasing daydreams, and may she be blessed with abundance—materially and spiritually.

Application: Visit a local fire station with your grandchild. Find out how well equipped firemen must be to do their jobs. They need special trucks, special hoses, special uniforms, and special training. Help your grandchild understand how she must use the "equipment" God has given her to do what He calls her to do.

September 22

"The wise woman builds her house,
but with her own hands
the foolish one tears hers down."

—Proverbs 14:1

Lord, I pray that my grandchild would be wise in building his life—not just his home, but every other aspect as well. Help him to understand that his character, his spirit, and his possessions are all gifts from You. Help him to care for them well and to use them wisely. I ask that You would keep foolishness from his life and help him to pursue Your wisdom in living.

Application: Find a large cardboard box and help your grandchild design a house out of the box. Draw the plans for the windows, doors, etc. As you work together, mention that he also needs to be careful when making decisions and plans for his life.

September 23

"She selects wool and flax
and works with eager hands."

—Proverbs 31:13

Father, I thank You for the creativity my grandchild is already displaying! It is amazing to see the abilities and talents You have woven into her life. Help her to delight in using her gifts and to experience joy as she develops them. Please let her never lose the wonder of watching You work through her life.

Application: Find a creative project to do with your grandchild: Draw or paint a picture, weave a potholder, build a birdhouse, etc. Remind your grandchild that her creativity is a gift from the Creator of all life.

September 24

"Be sure you know
the condition of your flocks,
give careful attention to your herds."

– Proverbs 27:23

Lord, You instruct us to know our flocks well—our children, our opportunities, our finances, our pets, our gardens. I pray that You would help my grandchild to be a diligent caretaker. Please help him not to take for granted the blessings You provide, but instead to watch over them carefully.

Application: Help your grandchild make some sheep out of construction paper and cotton balls. Talk about Jesus' statement in John 10: "I am the Good Shepherd." He knows who is in His family and how to take care of each one. He will protect and help those who believe in Him.

September 25

"In the paths of the wicked
lie thorns and snares,
but he who guards his soul
stays far from them."

—Proverbs 22:5

Lord, I pray that my grandchild would not follow the path of destruction and heartache which comes from associating with the wicked. Instead, I ask that You would help her to guard her heart and soul. Give her the courage to make the right choices. Help her to avoid all kinds of problems and temptations—"thorns and snares"—by caring for the gifts You have given her, gifts of faith, hope, and love.

Application: Read about the armor of God in Ephesians 6:13-18. Help your grandchild make a "shield of faith" out of cardboard or drawing paper. Talk about how her faith will protect her from making poor decisions and will help her guard her soul—become a good steward of the gifts God has placed within her.

September 26

"The plans of the diligent
lead to profit
as surely as haste
leads to poverty."

– Proverbs 21:5

Lord, thank You for this admonition to be diligent and to plan ahead, even when it often appears best to move swiftly without thinking. This proverb, however, assures us that such action leads only to poverty. Please help my grandchild to demonstrate patience, to use his time wisely, and to be a good steward of the skills, interests, and opportunities that You provide him.

Application: Choose a famous person that your grandchild admires—an athlete, an artist, a writer, etc. Together research this person—watch a movie, read a biography, or check out an Internet site—to discover more about the diligence and training required to develop his special skill.

September 27

"The lazy man will not plow
because of winter,
therefore he will beg during
the harvest and have nothing."

—Proverbs 20:4 (NKJV)

Lord, the warning in this proverb is that if there is not proper preparation, planning, and planting, there will be nothing to harvest. I pray that my grandchild would learn to take the proper measures to produce what she needs. I pray that she would know how to prepare and cultivate the fertile ground of faith so that much spiritual fruit can result from her work.

Application: Take your grandchild to a plant nursery or garden shop and talk to a gardener about the necessary procedures for growing flowers or a crop. Discuss how this demonstrates good stewardship of God's gifts—both physically and spiritually.

September 28

"The wealth of the rich
is their fortified city;
they imagine it
an unscalable wall."

– Proverbs 18:11

Father, although we know that You are the Source of all wealth and good things, it is sometimes tempting for us to put our trust in the gift rather than in the Giver. I pray that my grandchild would be a good steward of all that he has been given. Help him, however, not to be deceived into thinking that material goods can offer security. May he understand that the ultimate protection comes through a close relationship with You.

Application: Take your grandchild to a park where he can climb rocks, or to a climbing wall and let him practice rappelling. Discuss the truth of this proverb: Rich men may think they can depend upon their possessions, but God's Word tells us that riches are not a strong defense—*He* is our only safety.

September 29

"In the house of the wise
are stores of choice food and oil,
but a foolish man devours all he has."

—Proverbs 21:20

Father, being a good steward of Your gifts includes planning carefully for the future. I pray that my grandchild would wisely use, save, and share the gifts You have given her. Please bless her with enough to take care of herself, yet remain dependent on You. Help her to store sufficient provisions, in case of distress or disaster to be able to meet her own needs and to distribute a portion to others.

<u>Application:</u> Give your grandchild a small amount of money. Work out a budget together. Decide how much should be set aside for savings, how much for daily use, and how much for giving. Discuss how this will help her learn to be a good steward of her resources.

September 30

"From the fruit of his lips
a man is filled with good things
as surely as the work of his hands
rewards him."

—Proverbs 12:14

Lord, You call us to be stewards of both our words and our actions. I pray that my grandchild would choose his words carefully so that he would be well regarded and blessed. I also pray, Lord, that he would be diligent in the work You have provided him. Thank You that good stewardship both honors You and brings rewards to the steward.

Application: Help your grandchild understand that hard work can bring rewards. Find an age-appropriate task and ask your grandchild to accomplish it. Reward him with encouraging words, a treat, or a small monetary gift.

MAY MY GRANDCHILD LOVE...

HONESTY

OCTOBER

October 1

"Truthful lips endure forever,
but a lying tongue lasts only a moment."

--Proverbs 12:19

Truthful lips result from a heart surrendered to You. Lord, please help my grandchild to desire to know You well and to walk closely with You. I also pray that the words he speaks would have an everlasting impact for Your kingdom. Help him to understand that lying may feel good for the moment, but honesty is always the best policy.

Application: Read Isaiah 55:11 with your grandchild and explain that sharing God's Word with others always accomplishes His purposes. Remind him that God's Word is eternally true.

October 2

"Without wood a fire goes out;
without gossip a quarrel dies down."

— Proverbs 26:20

Father, the words we use carelessly can cause so much destruction. Like adding fuel to the fire, gossip promotes tension and division, especially if the information passed on is shaded so that it is no longer entirely true. I pray that my grandchild would have the wisdom and discernment to speak only the truth. May she understand that she can defuse a disagreement simply by not gossiping.

Application: Talk with your grandchild about wild fires that occur in many places across the world. Discuss how they destroy anything in their path unless firefighters create a clearing around the fire to reduce their "fuel." Mention that quarrels are fueled by gossip and hearsay and, without that type of fuel, the quarrels also die down.

October 3

"An honest answer
is like a kiss on the lips."

– Proverbs 24:26

Lord, Your Word often paints a down-to-earth picture—like this proverb. Not only is an honest answer the right response, it feels good. Help my grandchild to give and receive "honest answers." Help him to be amenable to instruction and correction. Let him understand that honesty is not only good for him, but also it is more valuable to hear the truth than a lie.

Application: Suggest to your grandchild: "Say something honest and kind to someone else that would make that person 'feel good'—feel affirmed and strengthened. But be sure you tell the truth!"

October 4

"A wicked man accepts a bribe in secret
to pervert the course of justice."

—Proverbs 17:23

Father, we may think that we can act secretly, but Your Word tells us that we cannot. You already know the intentions of our hearts and see all of our actions. I pray that my grandchild would not scheme in secret for the purpose of self-promotion. Help her to have honest intentions and to be willing to bear the consequences of poor decisions.

Application: Read Mark 14:10-11 and discuss how Judas schemed and plotted to betray Jesus in exchange for a bribe from the Pharisees.

October 5

"A wise man's heart guides his mouth, and his lips promote instruction."

—Proverbs 16:23

Lord, the words we speak can bring honor or insult to You. I pray that my grandchild would permit Your wisdom to permeate his life and guide his thoughts, words, and actions. Allow him to share his personal testimony of Your love openly and honestly so as to help and instruct others. May he be concerned about developing a "wise heart" so they will learn the truth about You.

Application: Work a crossword puzzle or word-find with your grandchild. Discuss the power of words and how many different meanings even one word can have.

October 6

"All a man's ways seem innocent to him, but motives are weighed by the LORD."

—PROVERBS 16:2

Father, thank You for giving us the Holy Spirit to bring conviction of sin, which allows us to repent so that You can replace our sinful motives with godly motives. Help my grandchild to surrender to You so that Your work can be completed in her. Gently teach her that Your ways are best. Please develop in her pure motives that result in honesty and integrity.

Application: Read the parable of the widow's mite in Luke 21:1-4. Explain to your grandchild that God knew this widow's heart and saw that her motivation was to honor Him. The size of her gift did not matter, but her dedication to God did.

October 7

"As charcoal to embers and as wood to fire, so is a quarrelsome man for kindling strife."

—Proverbs 26:21

Lord, I pray that my grandchild will not possess a quarrelsome temperament. It is apparent from this proverb that an argumentative spirit only results in disputes and accomplishes little. Let him seek to honestly understand all sides of a disagreement and to use his words for inspiration and healing.

Application: Discuss with your grandchild healthy ways to resolve disagreements. For example: Listen carefully to what the other person is saying. State your feelings using "I" sentences: "I feel angry that…." "I feel sad about…" Discuss how many disagreements can be resolved by understanding the perspective of everyone involved.

October 8

"What a man desires is unfailing love; better to be poor than a liar."

—Proverbs 19:22

Thank You, Lord, that Your Word always gives us Your pure perspective on life. Many people want what the world says they should have—wealth, prestige, status—and are willing to compromise what is right to achieve it. But Your Word tells us it is better to be poor than to sacrifice our standards. I pray, Lord, that my grandchild will stand firm in her convictions and never waver from a commitment to be truthful at all times.

Application: Retell the Bible story of Daniel (see Daniel 1:8-15). Discuss how God blessed Daniel when he didn't compromise his convictions and eat the king's food.

October 9

"Rich and poor have this in common:
the Lord is the Maker of them all."

—Proverbs 22:2

Father, at the end of our days, we will all face You. It won't matter if we were rich or poor, healthy or sick, white or black, educated or illiterate—what will matter is our faith in Jesus Christ and how we have lived it out. Help my grandchild to have an honest opinion of himself and to understand that all people are equal in Your sight. Help him to treat others fairly and to share his faith with everyone he meets.

<ins>Application:</ins> Sing the children's song together: "Jesus loves the little children, all the children of the world. Red and yellow, black and white, they are precious in His sight; Jesus loves the little children of the world."

October 10

"A truthful witness saves lives,
but a false witness is deceitful."

—Proverbs 14:25

Lord, Your Word calls us to be Your witnesses, and this proverb assures us that a truthful witness will save lives. I pray that my grandchild would be forthright and honest as she speaks with others about You. Help her to be willing to tell them what Jesus means to her so that her testimony will draw people to You. Thank You that You even use children to spread the good news of salvation.

Application: Read Acts 16:25-34 with your grandchild, showing what happened when Paul shared the gospel with his jailer. The whole family believed in Jesus!

October 11

"He whose walk is upright fears the LORD,
but he whose ways are devious
despises him."

—PROVERBS 14:2

Lord, this proverb reminds us that we "walk our talk." In other words, what we believe is demonstrated in how we live. I ask that my grandchild would be upright and maintain a healthy and awesome fear of You. Further, I pray that he would understand that devious ways expose a heart that has turned against You. Help him to choose his friends carefully and avoid relationships with individuals who have deceit in their hearts.

<u>Application:</u> Read the story of "Little Red Riding Hood" to your grandchild. Discuss the wolf's devious character. He was a liar and a trickster!

October 12

"The crucible for silver
and the furnace for gold,
but the LORD tests the heart."

—PROVERBS 17:3

Father, Your Word assures us that You will test our characters and the motives of our hearts. Your desire is to refine us so that our lives sincerely reflect You. I pray that my grandchild would not resist Your work, but that she would welcome it as a chance to become more like You.

Application: Share this short story with your grandchild: A woman went to a jeweler's shop to observe the process of refining silver. The jeweler held a piece of silver over a hot fire to burn away the impurities, watching carefully during the process. When the woman asked the jeweler how he knew when the silver was pure, he replied, "That's easy. I can see my reflection in the metal." God refines us, too, so that he can see His image in our lives.

October 13

"Do not plot harm against your neighbor,
who lives trustfully near you.
Do not accuse a man for no reason—
when he has done you no harm."

—Proverbs 3:29-30

Lord, I am so grateful that, through Your Word, You have shown my grandchild how to live peacefully with his neighbors. Help him not to wish them harm, but, instead, to bring them encouragement and kindness. Help him to represent Your love and grace as he lives an authentic and honest life in his community.

Application: From the story of Ruth in the Old Testament, explain to your grandchild how Boaz showed himself to be a kind, trustworthy, and honest neighbor as he provided not only for his relatives, Ruth and Naomi, but also for the poor in the community.

October 14

"It is not good to be partial to the wicked or to deprive the innocent of justice."

—Proverbs 18:5

Lord, I pray that You would guide my grandchild in all of her ways. Help her to treat all people impartially and justly. Encourage her to seek the truth and to demonstrate fairness in her decision-making. Do not allow her to be lured by temptations of evil or the desire to hurt others. Instead, help her to be a champion of justice.

Application: In an age-appropriate manner, talk with your grandchild about the court system and how it is designed to ensure justice for all people.

October 15

"A scoundrel and a villain, who goes about with a corrupt mouth, who winks with his eye, signals with his feet and motions with his fingers, who plots evil with deceit in his heart—he always stirs up dissension. Therefore disaster will overtake him in an instant; he will suddenly be destroyed—without remedy."

—Proverbs 6:12-15

Father, these words aptly describe a scheming, deceptive individual. It is evident that the results of such character traits are disastrous. I pray fervently that my grandchild would never become such a person, but would be a living demonstration of Your love. Protect him as he matures and enable him to live an honest and trustworthy life.

Application: Consult an encyclopedia or the Internet together for information on volcanoes. Discuss how quickly a volcano can erupt, sometimes after decades of inactivity. Help your grandchild to see that a corrupt life can appear calm and innocent for a time, but corruption inevitably leads to catastrophe.

October 16

"It is to a man's honor to avoid strife,
but every fool is quick to quarrel."

– Proverbs 20:3

Father, it takes discipline to control our angry reactions and avoid conflict and quarrels. I pray that You would develop that discipline in my grandchild. Help her to be wise in her response to others. May she not compromise her own beliefs, but express them honestly in a manner that is reflective of Your character in her.

Application: Read and discuss Ephesians 5:17 together: "Therefore do not be foolish, but understand what the Lord's will is." As you think about this proverb, consider what "the Lord's will" might be. One answer is found in the proverb.

October 17

"The LORD detests lying lips,
but He delights in men who are truthful."

—PROVERBS 12:22

Lord, I ask that You would delight in my grandchild. Help him to speak truth and not lies so that he can sense Your pleasure. Please make lying as detestable to him as it is to You. Develop in him a life of integrity so that he may represent You well.

Application: Read the story of "Pinocchio" to your grandchild. Discuss how the little puppet's nose grew when he lied. Share that we don't necessarily change physically when we lie, but lying does harm us in different ways. Dishonesty can change our character.

October 18

"Those who forsake the law
praise the wicked,
but those who keep the law
resist them."

--Proverbs 28:4

Father, help my grandchild to be a law-abiding citizen. Enable her to learn right from wrong, the truth from a lie, and good from evil. Help her, also, Lord, to know that Your Word issues us the highest calling and that our ultimate allegiance is not to an earthly leader, but to You.

Application: Read Jesus' words in Matthew 22:21: "Give to Caesar what is Caesar's, and to God what is God's." Discuss how we need to honor earthly laws, yet acknowledge that our foremost commitment is to the Lord.

October 19

"A fool's mouth is his undoing,
and his lips are a snare to his soul."

—PROVERBS 18:7

Lord, I pray that my grandchild would speak truthfully and honorably. Please keep him from saying things that would discredit You or damage his character. Since our actions reflect our beliefs, I ask that his choices would reveal a heart that desires to please You.

Application: Find some wax lips at a party store to give to your grandchild or draw big lips on him with lipstick or pencil. Talk about how foolish this looks and how the words that come from our lips can be foolish as well.

October 20

"A truthful witness does not deceive,
but a false witness pours out lies."

—Proverbs 14:5

Father, it is not honoring to You to deceive others with lies and trickery. I pray that my grandchild would be consistently honest in her walk with You. I ask that, as Your follower, she would be a witness to Your work in her life and in this world. Help her to speak the truth so that You will be glorified.

Application: Play an "icebreaker" game with your grandchild. Tell three things about yourself—two facts that are true; one, a lie. Point out how easy it is to deceive others and explain how God's Word warns us about lying.

October 21

"A violent man entices his neighbor
and leads him down a path
that is not good."

– Proverbs 16:29

Lord, please give my grandchild the privilege of leading others down a path toward You. Help him to know and proclaim the truth found in Scripture so that many will come to have a personal faith in Jesus Christ. Keep him from violent actions that only arouse anger and fear, and allow him to spread the peace of the gospel to a world that desperately needs hope and redemption.

Application: Teach your grandchild a rather simple gospel message to share with others: "God loves you. Every person has sinned. Jesus died for sinners." Then pray together that God would draw unbelievers to Himself.

October 22

"A truthful witness gives honest testimony, but a false witness tells lies."

—Proverbs 12:17

Lord, thank You for being a Righteous Judge who has set a high standard for how we are to speak. Help my grandchild to honor You by speaking with integrity. I pray, Lord, that she would tell the truth and nothing but the truth at all times, even when she is called to acknowledge something that is difficult. Thank You, Lord, for reminding us that the "word of our testimony" is powerful.

Application: Read Luke 1:35-38 with your grandchild. Discuss how Mary responded at a time of great difficulty. When she was frightened and uncertain as to what lay ahead, she affirmed her faith in God and glorified Him.

October 23

"Where there is no revelation,
the people cast off restraint;
but blessed is he who keeps the law."

—Proverbs 29:18

Father, I humbly thank You for the revelation in Your Word. You have given us all we need to live a life of faith. I pray that my grandchild would embrace Your truth and follow You. Help him to know the joy of a Spirit-filled and Christ-centered life.

Application: Discuss what happens when we break the law. If we drive through a red light in traffic, we may have an accident. If we swim in a "No Swimming" area, we may drown. But when we know what God wants us to do and are obedient, our lives are blessed.

October 24

"A scoundrel plots evil,
and his speech
is like a scorching fire."

—Proverbs 16:27

Lord, this proverb tells us that a scoundrel is an unprincipled person whose speech is as destructive as a raging fire! Please help my grandchild to refrain from such malicious behavior. May she learn to be honest, always regarding the truth with respect. Instead of using her words destructively, teach her to communicate encouragement and hope.

Application: On a piece of paper, randomly write some hurtful words. Help your grandchild color over them with a picture of flames to help her remember that these words can destroy.

October 25

"A fortune made by a lying tongue
is a fleeting vapor and a deadly snare."

—Proverbs 21:6

Lord, what the world offers is so attractive at times. We are often tempted to compromise our character in order to enjoy those pleasures. I pray that my grandchild would not be caught in the snare of success at the expense of godly convictions. I do ask, Lord, that he would understand how imperative it is to speak the truth and to live an honest life.

Application: Read the story of Shadrach, Meshach and Abednego (see Daniel 3:13-18). Ask your grandchild, "Would you be as brave as these three young men and tell the truth—even if it meant that you would be thrown into a fiery furnace?" Assure your grandchild that the Lord would also be with him in the midst of any trial, just as He was with these young men.

October 26

"He who keeps the law is a discerning son,
but a companion of gluttons
disgraces his father."

—Proverbs 28:7

Lord, discernment, like wisdom, is a gift from You. Develop in my grandchild the ability to choose good friends and to live her life as a law-abiding citizen. Purify her desires and motives. And, Lord, let her life reflect well on both her earthly family and her heavenly Father.

Application: Help your grandchild list the good choices she could make that would bring honor to her family.

October 27

"A hot-tempered man stirs up dissension, but a patient man calms a quarrel."

—Proverbs 15:18

Lord, every day we are faced with choices that will result in a life that either pleases or displeases You. We know that a quarrelsome and quick-tempered nature is not a reflection of Your love. I pray that my grandchild would be a patient person who honestly assesses all sides of a disagreement. Help him to recognize the value of harmony so that he will not carelessly sow seeds of discord.

Application: Practice with your grandchild ways to respond when you are involved in a controversy. One way might be to step back and calm yourself by breathing deeply; another might be to silently pray for God's wisdom for an appropriate response.

October 28

"Pride only brings quarrels,
but wisdom is found in those who take advice."

— Proverbs 13:10

Father, a prideful character is not pleasing to You. Pride often keeps us from the truth and brings disharmony in our relationship with others. I pray, Lord, that my grandchild would willingly take advice from godly individuals and that she would recognize pride as a trait that dishonors herself—and You.

Application: Discuss with your grandchild how prideful people act. For example, they may think that they are better than other people, or that they are above the law, or that they should be given special favors. Discuss, also, how pride can keep us from listening to good advice because we think we know better.

October 29

"The way of the guilty is devious,
but the conduct of the innocent is upright."

—Proverbs 21:8

Lord, we know that when we lie, our understanding of the truth can become warped. We then resort to devious and dishonest means to cover our guilt. I know that my grandchild is not perfect and that his sin nature will be evident at times. When that happens, please work in his heart and bring him to a point of repentance. Give him the joy of relying on Jesus for the forgiveness of sins and the restoration of his innocent ways.

Application: Share with your grandchild about a time when somebody lied to you, or you lied to someone else, and how you felt about it. Discuss what he should do when he catches himself or someone else in a lie.

October 30

"Kings take pleasure in honest lips;
they value a man who speaks the truth."

—Proverbs 16:13

Lord, we know that You prize truth and honesty so much that one of the names of Your Son is "Truth." This proverb suggests that even world leaders recognize the value of truthfulness. Lord, I pray that my grandchild would please You as well as others by always telling the truth.

Application: Help your grandchild make a card that contains a heartfelt and honest note of thanks to someone who has blessed her.

October 31

"He who loves a quarrel loves sin; he who builds a high gate invites destruction."

—Proverbs 17:19

Lord, this proverb teaches us that these two character traits—an argumentative spirit and a prideful lifestyle—are often interrelated. I pray that my grandchild would not be tempted by either one. I ask, Father, that he would learn to disagree in a respectful manner and not show a quarrelsome spirit. Help him to assess his own character honestly and to do his best to live in harmony with others.

Application: Find some building materials—blocks, Legos, popsicle sticks, etc. and build a house with a high wall and gate around it. Discuss how isolation and pride may erect walls that keep us from spreading God's love to those around us.

MAY MY GRANDCHILD DESIRE TO BE...

RIGHTEOUS

NOVEMBER

November 1

"When the righteous are in authority,
the people rejoice;
but when a wicked man rules,
the people groan."

—Proverbs 29:2 (NKJV)

Father, please provide righteous leadership in this country/state/city for my grandchild. Help her understand the importance of praying fervently for those in authority over her. May she rejoice and be thankful when she experiences life under righteous government. May she be so stirred by the actions of righteous leaders that she would also seek righteous living. Most of all, may she understand that You are sovereign over all and that You direct the affairs of men.

Application: The next time you participate in an election by voting, take your grandchild with you. Discuss beforehand why you want to support a righteous candidate.

November 2

"The Lord will not allow
the righteous soul to famish,
but he casteth away
the substance of the wicked."

– Proverbs 10:3 (NKJV)

Father, You are sovereign over all situations. There will be times when my grandchild will think that You have abandoned him to the desert. Please help him understand that such times are tremendous opportunities for growth and that You use them to help create in him a righteous character. May he know that "those who seek the Lord lack no good thing" (Psalm 34:10).

Application: Talk about a difficult time in your life when you thought God was far away, only to realize He was with you all the time.

November 3

"The wicked covet the catch of evil men, but the root of the righteous yields fruit."

—Proverbs 12:12 (NKJV)

Father, Your Word tells us that a tree is known by its fruit. Please help my grandchild's character to be so righteous that she will always bear good fruit. May she never envy or covet the gain of evildoers, but will instead trust that You know what is best for her and live out her life to Your glory.

Application: Walk through a grocery store and examine all the different types of fruit. Discuss the kinds of trees that produce such fruit. Share that God's Word says that righteousness in our lives will also produce fruit—such as love, joy, and peace.

November 4

"Wealth is worthless in the day of wrath, but righteousness delivers from death."

--Proverbs 11:4

Father, You are the Giver of all good things. I pray that my grandchild would always be thankful for the material blessings You have given him. Help him to understand, however, the transient nature of riches and never attempt to place his trust in them. May he know it is only by seeking first Your kingdom and righteousness that he will experience fullness of life.

Application: Read the parable of the rich man in Luke 12:16-21 and discuss how his riches did not save him from death. He gathered all his crops into a barn and was ready to celebrate his riches and security, but he did not live to enjoy them.

November 5

"The LORD is far from the wicked
but he hears the prayer of the righteous."

—PROVERBS 15:29

Father, thank You for the assurance that You hear the prayers of people who live righteously. I pray that my grandchild would accept the gift of Your Son and His righteousness and thus be able to turn to You with the confidence that You are listening. We are grateful that Jesus lives to make intercession on behalf of His children. Please frame my grandchild's heart and mind in such a way that prayers of thanksgiving will be an integral part of her life.

Application: Start a prayer list with your grandchild. Write the request, the date requested, and be sure to leave a space to fill in the day the Lord answered the prayer!

November 6

"In the way of righteousness there is life;
along that path is immortality."

—Proverbs 12:28

Father, Your Son Jesus is perfect righteousness and has fulfilled all the requirements of the Old Testament law. Thank You for the promise that "he who has the Son has life" (I John 5:12). I pray that my grandchild would never seek to satisfy You with a righteousness based on his own merit. Instead, may he accept Your gift of Jesus on his behalf, knowing that faith in Him is the path to eternal life.

Application: As you travel on a highway, discuss how obstacles on the road may be dangerous to drivers and need to be cleared. What are the obstacles in our lives that keep us from living righteously?

November 7

"For the LORD detests a perverse man
but takes the upright into his confidence."

—PROVERBS 3:32

Father, thank You for calling us to be Your chosen people and revealing Yourself to us. Please develop in my grandchild the uprightness of heart and mind to be able to discern spiritual truths. I pray that she will understand the incredible privilege she has been given to know You intimately as her personal Savior. As she matures in her faith, may she come to know the great joy of being Your confidante, one whom You trust with Your secrets!

Application: Ask your grandchild with whom he would like to share his secrets. It will probably be someone he trusts and knows well. This proverb says that God will share His secrets with those who know and love Him.

November 8

"The desire of the righteous
ends only in good,
but the hope of the wicked only in wrath."

—Proverbs 11:23

Father, I pray that the desires of my grandchild will always be focused on You. May his actions be motivated by that which is "true, noble, right, pure, lovely, admirable, excellent and praiseworthy" (Philippians 4:8). As he matures in his understanding of You and Your love, may his life reflect an eager anticipation of all the good You have for him in Christ Jesus.

Application: Give a gift to your grandchild. Discuss how we can also expect good gifts from God because of His great love for us.

November 9

"The house of the righteous
contains great treasure,
but the income of the wicked
brings them trouble."

—Proverbs 15:6

Father, You bless Your people lavishly with infinite treasure. Please help my grandchild understand that "treasure" comes in many forms—frequently spiritual rather than material. May she recognize that the greatest treasure she will ever possess is Your righteousness, given as a free gift through grace and faith in the Lord Jesus. Thank You for the promise that this treasure is stored in heaven and is eternally protected.

Application: Hide "treasures" around your house. Then go on a treasure hunt with your grandchild. Discuss the different types of treasures God gives us—both material and spiritual.

November 10

"The lips of the righteous nourish many,
but fools die for lack of judgment."

—Proverbs 10:21

Father, I pray that my grandchild would be so saturated with Your love that when he speaks, others would be encouraged. Help him to understand the power of the Scriptures. Give him the understanding that Your Word spoken through him "will not return void," but will accomplish Your divine purposes (see Isaiah 55: 11). Please continue to work in him to create a righteous life that brings spiritual nourishment to many others.

Application: Bake some bread with your grandchild. Discuss the fact that bread is necessary to physical life and health. Then talk about Jesus, the Bread of Life, and how He is essential to one's spiritual life.

November 11

"The righteous eat to their hearts' content, but the stomach of the wicked goes hungry."

—Proverbs 13:25

Father, You have created us with a hunger for both spiritual and physical food. Please give my grandchild the desire to satisfy her appetite with those things that will be most nourishing for her. Help her to desire righteousness so that she may "taste and see that the Lord is good." Thank You that our contentment and satisfaction are found in You.

Application: Discuss the consequences of making poor food choices. When we do not eat well, we become weak, ill, or unhealthy. Share how we can also make poor choices for our soul—we can disregard God's Word, choose the wrong friends, neglect worship, etc.

November 12

"The path of the righteous
is like the first gleam of dawn,
shining ever brighter
till the full light of day."

—Proverbs 4:18

Lord, thank You for sending Jesus to be light in a dark and confused world. As my grandchild grows in his understanding of You, please enable him to reflect Your righteousness and love. Reveal to him those areas of his life needing the purifying power of the gospel, and use him to bring light and clarity to the lives of others.

Application: Show your grandchild how one small light (candle or flashlight) can make a difference in a dark room. Compare this light with the difference a Christian can make in the darkness of a troubled world.

November 13

"The thoughts of the righteous are right,
but the counsels of the wicked are deceitful."

—Proverbs 12:5 (NKJV)

Father, I pray that You would work in the mind of my grandchild. Please give her the desire to study and meditate on Your Word so that her thoughts would be transformed by Your power. Give her the discernment to recognize deceitful counselors and to seek instead those who love You and are righteous in thought and action.

Application: Memorize with your grandchild Romans 12:2: "Do not conform any longer to the pattern of this world, but be transformed by the renewing of your mind. Then you will be able to test and approve what God's will is—his good, pleasing and perfect will."

November 14

"The heart of the righteous
studies how to answer,
but the mouth of the wicked
pours forth evil."

—Proverbs 15:28 (NKJV)

Father, I commend the heart and mind of my grandchild to You. Please help him to studiously prepare so that he will be ready to give an answer to everyone who asks about the hope that he has (see 1 Peter 3:15).

Application: Demonstrate to your grandchild the importance of *how* we say things and not just *wha*t we say. Repeat the sentence below, each time emphasizing the underlined word and see how your grandchild reacts to each one:

I didn't say you had an attitude problem.
I didn't say you had an attitude problem.
I didn't say you had an attitude problem.

November 15

"Even a child is known by his actions,
by whether his conduct is pure and right."

—Proverbs 20:11

Father, Jesus tenderly picked up little children in His arms and blessed them. I pray that my grandchild would understand how important she is to You. Please help her appreciate the power her words and deeds can have in promoting Your kingdom. Help her to desire to do what is pure and right.

Application: Share the truth of this proverb with your grandchild: Even children develop a reputation for what they do. Think of some "actions" to do together that would demonstrate a pure and loving spirit—and then do them!

November 16

"The memory of the righteous
will be a blessing,
but the name of the wicked will rot."

—Proverbs 10:7

Father, You are the God who gives the gift of memories. Please help my grandchild know that a life lived in Your presence will be a life well remembered. I pray specifically that he will want to be remembered as a righteous person who loved and followed You. May he leave a legacy of faithfulness that blesses others.

Application: Start a memory book/scrapbook with your grandchild. Fill it with pictures, program bulletins, written work, etc. that are memories of his spiritual journey. This will help him to understand and visualize the legacy he can leave for others.

November 17

"When calamity comes,
the wicked are brought down,
but even in death the righteous
have a refuge."

—Proverbs 14:32

Father, the resurrection of Jesus is a vivid picture of our refuge in death. Please help my grandchild know that she does not need to be fearful of death if she has accepted Jesus' righteousness on her behalf. Help her understand that Jesus has gone before us, not only to conquer death, but to prepare an eternal home for us in heaven.

Application: Describe to your grandchild some of the glories of heaven as seen in Chapters 21 and 22 of the Book of Revelation: Everything will be new; there will be no more tears; we will need no sun or light because God's glory will illuminate the world.

November 18

"Wicked men are overthrown
and are no more,
but the house of the righteous
stands firm."

—Proverbs 12:7

Father, You are the Creator and Sustainer of all the world. Please help my grandchild see that You alone are the only permanent foundation upon which he can build his life. Help him know that unless his house is built on You—grounded on faith—he builds in vain. May he have the assurance that a righteous life secured on a godly foundation lasts forever.

Application: Make sand castles in a sandbox or on a beach. Demonstrate how water will destroy a house built with sand because it doesn't have a strong foundation. Share how this reminds us that our lives will be easily destroyed if we don't have a firm foundation of faith.

November 19

"When the storm has swept by,
the wicked are gone,
but the righteous stand firm forever."

—Proverbs 10:25

Father, I pray that You will establish a righteous foundation within my grandchild that will not be shaken. As she experiences the storms of affliction and suffering, enable her to cling to the only One who can rebuke and calm the winds of life. Help her to understand that it is not her strength, but Yours, that will take her through the hard times.

<u>Application:</u> Find books in the library (or resources on the Internet) about storms and tornadoes. Discuss how the power of the Creator is infinitely stronger than the mightiest storm.

November 20

"The name of the LORD is a strong tower; the righteous run to it and are safe."

—PROVERBS 18:10

Jehovah, Your very name means that You have the power to save Your people. Please work in the life of my grandchild in such a way that he will look to You alone as his refuge and protection. May there never be a day in his life, no matter what the circumstance, that he does not find his righteousness in Jesus and experience His peace.

Application: Share with your grandchild some of the many biblical names used for God and what they mean. Some examples are: Jehovah/Yahweh—"Self-Existent One"; El Shaddai—"God Almighty or God Is Sufficient"; Adonai—"Master or Lord"; Jehovah-Jireh—"The Lord Will Provide."

November 21

"The righteousness of the upright
delivers them,
but the unfaithful
are trapped by evil desires."

— Proverbs 11:6

Father, this proverb contrasts the ways of the righteous with the ways of the unfaithful. I pray that my grandchild would believe this truth and seek to be guided by You in the way of righteousness. Please help her understand that you have ordered the world in such a way that by following Your instructions, she will be able to overcome temptation.

Application: Read the story of Jesus in the desert (Matthew 4:1-11) to your grandchild. Show her how He used the Word of God to resist the devil. Let her know how important it is to know God's Word so we can discern right from wrong—and not be trapped by "evil desires."

November 22

"The Lord detests the way of the wicked,
but he loves those
who pursue righteousness."

—Proverbs 15:9

Lord, Your Word assures us that You have the same love for us that You have for Your Son Jesus. I ask that my grandchild would accept Jesus as his Savior and pursue—run after—a righteous life. Help him never tire of hearing that You, the Mighty One, rejoice over him with gladness and singing (see Zephaniah 3:17).

Application: Sing with your grandchild the song, "Jesus Loves Me This I Know."

November 23

"Whoever trusts in his riches will fall,
but the righteous will thrive
like a green leaf."

—Proverbs 11:28

Father, please help my grandchild not to trust in the riches of this world. May she understand that her greatest fulfillment will come in living a life of righteousness through You. Do not allow her to be distracted by the enticements of this world, but please draw close to her and let her flourish as she humbly obeys Your Word.

Application: Take a walk in the park or woods and look at the trees and foliage. Coniferous trees will still be flourishing, but other types of trees may have lost their leaves. Share how God wants His righteousness to flourish in you all year long.

November 24

"A man cannot be established
through wickedness,
but the righteous cannot be uprooted."

— PROVERBS 12:3

Father, we clearly see from your design in nature, whether the smallest flower or the tallest tree, how essential a strong root system is to growth and stability. I pray that my grandchild would be deeply rooted and grounded in the love of Christ so that his life would be one of righteousness. May these deep roots of faith be able not only to withstand the strongest of trials and temptations, but actually be strengthened by them.

Application: Demonstrate or describe to your grandchild how difficult it is to dig up a tree stump with deep roots. Discuss why the root system is crucial to plants and trees and how this illustrates why growing deep in our faith in God sustains us during difficult times.

November 25

"The wicked man earns deceptive wages,
but he who sows righteousness
reaps a sure reward."

—Proverbs 11:18

Father, we sometimes become discouraged when our work does not appear to have lasting value. I pray specifically that You will impress upon my grandchild Your promise that her labor is not in vain and that work directed by You has eternal purpose. May she desire to hear the words of affirmation from the parable of the sower in Matthew 25: "Well done, my good and faithful servant."

Application: Make a list of actions that demonstrate a righteous life such as loving the unlovable, helping others, knowing God's Word. Discuss what "rewards" your grandchild might hope for if she lived this kind of life (joy, satisfaction, strong relationships, etc.).

November 26

"The way of the LORD
is a refuge for the righteous."

– PROVERBS 10:29A

Father, we know that Your ways are perfect and higher than our ways. I pray that my grandchild would always desire to seek You and Your direction for his life. I ask that Your Spirit would enable him to live a life of goodness and righteousness. Thank You for being his refuge and strength as he obeys and follows You.

Application: Read the book or watch the movie, *The Wizard of Oz,* with your grandchild. Discuss how the Yellow Brick Road was the "way" Dorothy and her friends followed to reach the city of Oz. The "Way" to God is His Son, Jesus.

November 27

"The Lord detests the sacrifice of the wicked, but the prayer of the upright pleases Him."

—Proverbs 15:8

Father, please create in my grandchild a heart which longs for communion with You. I ask that she never waver in bringing her every prayer boldly to Your throne of grace. May spending time with You be a top priority in her life. Please encourage her by Your Spirit to desire to live an upright life so that her prayers will please You.

Application: Teach your grandchild the method of prayer based on the acronym ACTS: **A**doration, **C**onfession, **T**hanksgiving, and **S**upplication.

November 28

"The fruit of the righteous is a tree of life, and he who wins souls is wise."

—Proverbs 11:30

Father, You are the Lord of the harvest, both physically and spiritually. Please work in my grandchild in such a way that his life will produce living fruit—"love, joy, peace, patience, kindness, goodness, faithfulness, gentleness, and self-control" (Galatians 5:22). I pray that these characteristics will overflow as a witness to others who will then be drawn to You.

Application: Take your grandchild to an orchard, farm, or local market and look at the fruit. Choose a fruit to represent each of the different fruit of the Spirit—i.e., an apple for love, an orange for joy, a pear for peace, a peach for patience, a banana for kindness, a cherry for goodness, a strawberry for faithfulness, a blueberry for gentleness and a kiwi for self-control. This will help your grandchild to remember God's work in his life.

November 29

"The LORD's curse
is on the house of the wicked,
but he blesses the home of the righteous."

—PROVERBS 3:33

Father, thank You for redeeming Your people from the curse of the law. Please enable my grandchild to fully understand that only Christ's perfect obedience could satisfy the demands of the law. When she accepts Him as her personal Savior, He gives her a new heart that desires to follow Him. Help her to live a righteous life rooted in grace and not in performance. May she delight in the blessings promised to her through the righteousness of Jesus.

Application: Draw two tablets on a large sheet of paper and write the Ten Commandments on those tablets (see Exodus 20:1-17). Talk to your grandchild about the fact that no one could perfectly keep those laws, so God sent Jesus Christ to fulfill the law on our behalf.

November 30

"Righteousness exalts a nation,
but sin is a disgrace
to any people."

—Proverbs 14:34

Father, this world has been the recipient of countless blessings from You. I pray that my grandchild would never take those blessings for granted. May he use his freedom in You to do what is good and beneficial for others. Please impress upon him the impact one righteous person can have on a whole community and ultimately a nation.

Application: Find and share information on an individual of faith who has had an impact on his or her nation. An example might be William Wilberforce, who led the movement to abolish slavery in England.

MAY MY GRANDCHILD SEEK...

WISDOM

DECEMBER

December 1

"Wise men store up knowledge,
but the mouth of a fool invites ruin."

—Proverbs 10:14

Lord, encourage my grandchild to seek to know You—Your Word and Your ways. Please do not allow him to ruin his life by speaking foolishly. Instead, help him to be wise by storing up knowledge, studying Scripture, memorizing Bible verses, and being inspired by men and women of great faith.

Application: Read the following nursery rhyme about an owl and discuss the need to speak wisely:

A wise old owl sat in an oak,
The more he heard, the less he spoke;
The less he spoke, the more he heard;
Why aren't we all like that wise old bird?

December 2

"My son,
preserve sound judgment and discernment,
do not let them out of your sight;
they will be life for you."

—Proverbs 3:21-22a

Lord, I pray that my grandchild would be careful to safeguard her good judgment and discerning mind. Help her not to be distracted by the ways of the world. Allow her to know truth from lies and wisdom from folly. Please, Lord, preserve her life through her relationship with You.

Application: Take a short car ride with your grandchild. As you "buckle up for safety," share how this is one means of protecting and preserving our lives. Point out that this proverb also reminds us to use "sound judgment and discernment" for our spiritual protection.

December 3

"By wisdom a house is built,
and through understanding it is established;
through knowledge its rooms are filled
with rare and beautiful treasures."

—Proverbs 24:3

Lord, the treasures of this world are only temporary. At the end of our lives, all of our material belongings will be of no benefit to us. I pray that my grandchild would fill his life with treasures that are eternal. Help his home to be built on spiritual wisdom and understanding. May his life be lived in such a way that the knowledge of You and Your Word are his most valued possessions.

Application: Take your grandchild to a local dump or junkyard. Look at all the possessions that have been discarded. They were once someone's treasures, but now they are no longer valuable.

December 4

"A fool finds pleasure in evil conduct,
but a man of understanding
delights in wisdom."

—Proverbs 10:23

Father, it seems that the world today frequently endorses evil over good; people are rewarded for their antics and applauded for their immorality. I ask that wicked behavior would have no appeal for my grandchild. Please help her to find pleasure in conduct that is pleasing to You. Allow her to be a wise woman whose joy comes from knowing and doing Your will.

Application: Tell your grandchild that you would like to share a cookie with her. Put the cookie on the counter and tell her that she can cut it, but you will choose the first piece. State how it might be tempting to be greedy when sharing, but when we know the whole picture, or story, we would rather be wise.

December 5

"Get wisdom, get understanding;
do not forget my words
or swerve from them."

—PROVERBS 4: 5

Father, please give my grandchild the desire to be wise and understanding. Help him to receive Your Spirit of wisdom and revelation so that he may know You better (see Ephesians 1:17). I pray that his path in life would not be characterized by foolishness, but instead would be marked by wise choices. Help him not to swerve from Your words of wisdom as found in Scripture, but to remain true to their calling.

Application: Read 1 Kings 3:16-23 to your grandchild. In the story of the two mothers with one living child between them, ask how he would decide which woman was the real mother. Then read the rest of the story in verses 24-28, showing King Solomon's wise decision.

December 6

"Discretion will protect you,
and understanding will guard you."

—Proverbs 2:11

Lord, as my grandchild walks through this sometimes dangerous world, I pray that she will be protected with the armor of discretion and understanding. Please don't let foolish fancies and irresponsibility break through that armor, but let her hold firm to the knowledge of You. Thank You for always watching over her.

Application: Tell your grandchild the story of Rahab from Joshua 2. Using a large piece of white paper and crayons, draw a mural together of the events of this story. Emphasize that Rahab understood what God wanted her to do and she was protected because of her good judgment.

December 7

"The way of a fool seems right to him,
but a wise man listens to advice."

—Proverbs 12:15

Father, please don't allow my grandchild to be so stubborn that he won't listen to advice. I pray that he would wisely seek the counsel of others and would carefully consider what they have to say. Help him to be strong in his commitments and knowledgeable about what he believes, but humble enough to know that the perspectives and experiences of others can enrich his life.

Application: Read to your grandchild the story of Moses, who listened to the wise advice of his father-in-law, Jethro (see Exodus 18). No matter how strong our faith, there is value in paying attention to the wisdom and counsel of others.

December 8

"For the LORD gives wisdom,
and from his mouth
come knowledge and understanding."

—Proverbs 2:6

Father, thank You for Your promise that if we lack wisdom, all we need to do is ask and You will give it generously (see James 1:5). I am certain that my grandchild will need Your wisdom and guidance on a daily basis. Please help me to encourage her to ask for it, then to expect the answer to her prayer. As You have promised, I know You will provide generously.

Application: Take a trip to the local library and look at the thousands of books in the stacks. Share with your grandchild that though these books represent the knowledge of the world, there is only one Book that contains the wisdom of God—the Holy Bible.

December 9

"A wise son brings joy to his father,
but a foolish man despises his mother."

—Proverbs 15:20

Father, please allow my grandchild to be a delight to his parents. I pray that he would both admire his mother and bring joy to his father. Help him to be wise and not foolish so that his parents can be thankful for his good choices. May his family relationships be harmonious and ultimately a testimony to his commitment to You.

Application: With your grandchild, think of some things he could do that would bring joy to his father and demonstrate love to his mother. Encourage him to choose one activity for each of his parents and complete them.

December 10

"The wise in heart are called discerning, and pleasant words promote instruction."

—Proverbs 16:21

Lord, please help my grandchild to learn effective communication skills. Teach her to choose words that will convey affirmation and acceptance of others. Give her the wisdom to speak truth so that those who hear would mature and grow in their faith. Enable her to discern their needs so that she will be able to point them to Your sufficiency.

Application: Make signs of "kindness words" on construction paper with magic markers. Write such phrases as "I will pray for you," "God loves you," and "You are my friend." Then attach them with a magnet to the refrigerator to remind your grandchild to use "pleasant words."

December 11

"Buy the truth and do not sell it;
get wisdom, discipline and understanding.
The father of a righteous man has great joy;
he who has a wise son delights in him."

– Proverbs 23:23-24

"Where your treasure is, there your heart will be also" is a truth that we learn from Jesus (see Matthew 6:21). I pray that my grandchild would prize understanding and wisdom above material wealth. Help him hold fast to the certainties of his faith and not compromise his beliefs for a momentary and fleeting pleasure.

Application: Look at a picture of an owl with your grandchild and talk about why owls are considered "wise." Is it because they have big eyes and seem like they can see everything? Is it because they are nocturnal creatures and can hunt in the dark? Is it because they can fly soundlessly? We don't know exactly the reason owls are considered wise, but we know that we can be wise if we seek God's wisdom.

December 12

"The discerning heart seeks knowledge, but the mouth of a fool feeds on folly."

—Proverbs 15:14

"Garbage in, garbage out!" This is a contemporary version of an old adage—what we put into our minds often comes out of our mouths! I pray that my grandchild would fill her mind with knowledge of You and Your Word instead of anything foolish. Then, Lord, please allow her words and actions to reflect a discerning heart and knowledge of her Savior.

Application: Share a meal or snack and talk about how we need not only to feed our bodies, but our minds. Let your grandchild know that if she "feeds" her mind and heart with the things of God, she will become a very wise young person.

December 13

"The purposes of a man's heart
are deep waters,
but a man of understanding
draws them out."

—Proverbs 20:5

Father, sometimes we do not seem to know our own hearts. Yet this proverb tells us that someone who understands can draw out the purposes of others. How amazing to realize that a person's true motives and intentions can be examined. Lord, please equip my grandchild with the skills to bring clarity in times of confusion. Allow him to minister to others by helping them understand the deep issues of their hearts.

Application: Take your grandchild to visit an aquarium. Explain that, like the sea life that is hidden in deep waters, we sometimes don't even know the intentions of our own hearts. But God will help us to understand Him and, in the process, better understand ourselves and others.

December 14

"A rebuke impresses a man of discernment more than a hundred lashes a fool."

—Proverbs 17:10

Father, please give my grandchild the wisdom to understand that criticism can be constructive. Give her the ability to discern the difference between what is beneficial and what is hurtful. I pray that she would be willing to receive the help that comes from objective insight. Keep her from demonstrating a stubbornness that prohibits the gaining of wisdom.

Application: In a newspaper or on the Internet, read a critic's analysis of a restaurant, book, or movie. Explain that these critics have earned the respect of others by delivering critical analyses that benefit both the artist and the consumer.

December 15

"He who trusts in himself is a fool,
but he who walks in wisdom
is kept safe."

—Proverbs 28:26

Lord, this world can be a scary place. We can even feel afraid in our own homes or neighborhoods. Please, Lord, keep my grandchild safely in Your care. Impress upon him the need to trust in You and not in himself. Erase any fear from his life and give him the wisdom and assurance that You are always with him and will never leave him or forsake him (see Hebrews 13:5).

Application: Memorize Hebrews 13:5 together: "Never will I leave you; never will I forsake you."

December 16

"A man of knowledge
uses words with restraint,
and a man of understanding
is even-tempered."

– Proverbs 17:27

Father, I pray that my grandchild would be calm and even-tempered. Help her not to be easily angered or vengeful, but instead to pursue peace. Give her the wisdom to choose her words carefully and the knowledge that she cannot take them back once they are spoken. Let her conversation reflect a restraint that You are developing within her.

Application: Find and read a copy of the Gettysburg Address written and delivered by Abraham Lincoln in 1863. In this very short (one-and-a-half minute) speech, President Lincoln effectively demonstrated how to deliver a powerful message while using restraint.

December 17

"Gold there is, and rubies in abundance,
but lips that speak knowledge
are a rare jewel."

—Proverbs 20:15

Father, please refine my grandchild like a rare jewel; allow him to be valued by others because of his ability to speak knowledgably. Help him to think before he speaks and to understand the impact of his words. Please give him the wisdom to communicate just the right perspective, information, encouragement, or admonition. Help him also to cherish this gift of wisdom and to value it more than the most precious possessions of this world.

Application: Visit a jewelry store with your grandchild and look at all the rare and valuable jewels. While you are admiring them, share how this proverb states that words of wisdom are even more rare and valuable.

December 18

"He who walks with the wise
grows wise,
but a companion of fools
suffers harm."

—Proverbs 13:20

Lord, Your Word tells us that we come to resemble those with whom we associate. I ask, Lord, that you keep my grandchild from foolish friends and help her choose those who are wise. Bless her with role models—parents, teachers, leaders—who live lives committed to You.

Application: Read 1 Corinthians 15:33 together: "Bad company corrupts good character." Ask your grandchild what she thinks this might mean.

December 19

"Like a gold ring in a pig's snout
is a beautiful woman
who shows no discretion."

—Proverbs 11:22

Lord, this proverb is another humorous depiction of the result of poor choices. How odd a pig with a gold ring in its snout would look! I pray that my grandchild would show discretion in all that he does. Help him to live responsibly and make decisions that will be respected. I ask that he not be noticed for his antics, but instead would cultivate a reputation based on a circumspect walk with You.

Application: With your grandchild, make a mask out of a paper plate. Draw a silly face on it. Then punch holes on the sides and attach string or ribbon to tie it around your head. Laugh about how silly this looks, but state that looks are so deceiving. What is truly attractive is a life lived wisely.

December 20

"Understanding is a fountain of life
to those who have it,
but folly brings punishment to fools."

—Proverbs 16:22

Father, please cause my grandchild to bubble over with the joy that comes from wisdom and understanding. Help her to know the Source of all life, Jesus Himself. May she be a diligent student of Scripture and drink deeply from its truths. Enable her to live a devoted, disciplined life so that she can dwell abundantly in Your love.

Application: Prepare a bubble bath for your grandchild. Tell her that when she sees bubbles, she can remember that God's wisdom bubbles up like a fountain and gives joyful, abundant life.

December 21

"A prudent man sees danger
and takes refuge,
but the simple keep going
and suffer for it."

—Proverbs 22:3

Warnings of danger are sometimes very clear—a siren indicating bad weather or a flashing light signifying an accident ahead—but the dangers in life rarely are so apparent. I pray that my grandchild would have the ability to see the dangers ahead and would not just "keep going and suffer for it." Please give him the wisdom to seek safety in the midst of peril. Bless him with the knowledge that he can always find his peace, comfort, and rest in You.

Application: Discuss what you would do if you heard a severe weather warning. Would you move to a protected room? Move to the basement? A wise person learns to be prepared for possible dangers ahead.

December 22

"How much better to get wisdom than gold,
to choose understanding rather than silver."

—Proverbs 16:16

Father, we have many choices in this world today. It is tempting to choose something of material value rather than spiritual value. Your Word (see Luke 10:38-42) tells us that Mary made the better choice by sitting at the feet of Jesus and listening to what He said. I pray that my grandchild would make the same choice—pursuing an understanding of God that reaps everlasting value.

Application: Hide some coins around a room and ask your grandchild to help dust that room. Let her find and keep the coins, then discuss with her that although these are valuable, it is so much better to be wise than wealthy.

December 23

"The teaching of the wise
is a fountain of life,
turning a man
from the snares of death."

—PROVERBS 13:14

Father, thank You for the promise in John 7:38 that Your Spirit will be "streams of living water," flowing within believers. I ask that this would be the wisdom that courses through my grandchild's life. Please allow Your wisdom to guide him into activities that enhance his life rather than destroy it. Help him to see that he can turn to You at any time for direction and support.

Application: Research organizations that are digging wells for communities across the world—Samaritan's Purse, World Vision, local charities, churches or synagogues. Discuss how water sustains life and brings hope to the people. The Holy Spirit, like deep wells or flowing streams, provides us with refreshment and hope.

December 24

"The mocker seeks wisdom
and finds none,
but knowledge comes easily
to the discerning."

— Proverbs 14:6

Lord, please let discernment and knowledge be hallmarks of my grandchild's life. Make her receptive to learning about You and Your Word. Don't allow her activities to distract her from an intentional pursuit of wisdom, but let her life reflect her desire for more of You. Give her a passion to be a lifelong learner of spiritual truths.

Application: Share something new you have learned in the last year. Talk about how valuable it is to be a lifelong learner and ask your grandchild how she can continue to learn about wisdom, knowledge, and discernment.

December 25

"My son, if your heart is wise,
then my heart will be glad;
my inmost being will rejoice
when your lips speak what is right."

—Proverbs 23:15-16

Lord, thank You for sending Your Son, our Savior, Jesus, whose birthday we celebrate on this day. For parents and grandparents, few things bring us greater joy than our children's wise choices and love of truth. So we also know that Your Son's obedient life was well pleasing to You. I pray that my grandchild would always make the hearts of his parents glad by speaking truth and doing what is right.

Application: Bake a birthday cake for Jesus to help observe this holiday. While celebrating, share how God's gift of ...s Son was the greatest gift ever given. Remind him that ...lievers around the world rejoice like the heavenly ...hat first Christmas Day—and like the heart of His ...n He walked in perfect truth.

December 26

"A rich man may be wise in his own eyes, but a poor man who has discernment sees through him."

—Proverbs 28:11

Lord, please give my grandchild wisdom before success and discernment before wealth. Help her to be an excellent judge of character and to know the truth when she hears it. Do not allow her to be persuaded by fine words and convincing arguments that would lead her astray. Whether she is rich or poor, please keep her humble and wise.

Application: Talk about X-rays with your grandchild and how they can "see" right through our skin. Discuss how this proverb tells us that a person who is wise and discerning can "see through" the motives of others.

December 27

"A fool spurns his father's discipline,
but whoever heeds correction
shows prudence."

—Proverbs 15:5

Father, please encourage my grandchild's parents to seek You for direction and guidance in their home. Allow them to convey love and discipline in the Spirit of Christ. I pray that my grandchild would be receptive to their teaching. Help him to wisely accept godly correction, then help him to grow spiritually as a result.

Application: Tell your grandchild's parents that you are praying for them and that you appreciate the difficulty of bringing up children in this sinful world. Be sure to let your grandchild know that you are praying for his parents to have wisdom to lead their family in a way that is pleasing to You.

December 28

"Folly delights a man who lacks judgment,
but a man of understanding
keeps a straight course."

–Proverbs 15:21

Lord, please help my grandchild not to be attracted by folly or foolishness. Help her to understand the futility of such pursuit. Instead, I pray that she would learn to make wise decisions about the direction she should take in life. Help her to mature in the gifts and talents You have given her and to stay on a course that glorifies you.

Application: Affirm your grandchild by describing a gift or talent that you have observed in her and discuss how she can use it to God's glory.

December 29

"Know also that wisdom
is sweet to your soul; if you find it,
there is a future hope for you,
and your hope will not be cut off."

—Proverbs 24:14

Chocolate may seem sweet to my grandchild, Lord, but I'm afraid he might not yet understand how sweet wisdom is to his soul. I pray that You would enable him to understand and—like a chocolate treat—want more of it! The hope that comes from a relationship with You cannot be taken from him and will cause him to delight in Your promises for his future.

Application: Eat something sweet with your grandchild and talk about how quickly that sweetness is gone. Tell him that the sweetness we receive from knowing God will never leave us, giving us hope for the future.

December 30

"The lips of the wise spread knowledge;
not so the hearts of fools."

—Proverbs 15:7

Thank You, Lord, for helping us to understand that what we say often reflects who we are. I pray that my grandchild's speech would reveal a deep love for You. Please fill her with Your wisdom so that she can encourage and direct others in faith. Allow her heart to be dedicated to the pursuit of goodness and not foolishness.

Application: Tell your grandchild the story of "Chicken Little." When an acorn dropped on her head, she rushed to tell the king, "The sky is falling!" How did this reaction spread foolishness and not wisdom?

December 31

"Mockers stir up a city,
but wise men turn away anger."

—Proverbs 29:8

Lord, it is Your wisdom alone that can bring unity to this world. As we end this year, I ask that Your peace might reign in the earth. Help my grandchild to have a part in "turning away" the anger of others. Please allow him the privilege of being a peacemaker through sharing Your wisdom that points to the Prince of Peace, Jesus.

Application: Sit next to your grandchild and hold hands. Together thank the Lord for this year and pray for God's wisdom, peace, and glory to reign in the coming year.

Kathy

Kathryn March is a wife, mother, and grandmother. She and her husband, Sal, have been married for 35 years. They have two married children and two young granddaughters. Kathy grew up in Minnesota and presently lives in Brentwood, Tennessee. Her undergraduate degree is from Wells College and she has a Masters Degree in Counseling from Minnesota State University at Mankato. She has been involved in church ministries for more than 30 years and has a special heart for missions and women's ministry. Kathy has spoken at both national and international ministry conferences. Presently, she works as an educational and career advisor to students and young adults. She is also an avid runner, having completed two marathons, and she enjoys sharing a good cup of coffee with friends.

Pam

A child of the Mississippi Delta, Pam Ferriss grew up in Mississippi and Louisiana. She received a degree in political science from Mississippi State University and a Juris Doctor degree from the University of Mississippi. Pam has been married to David for 33 years; they have two married children. She is also a grandmother to two young granddaughters. She presently divides her time between Simsbury, Connecticut, and Nashville, Tennessee, where she is active as a community and church volunteer. She especially enjoys studying theology, teaching the Scriptures, and ministering to mothers with young children. While reading, gardening, and hiking are a few of her favorite pastimes, her all-time favorite "hobby" is to connect people with each other.

Susan

Susan is a native of Louisiana and graduated with a degree in psychology from Louisiana State University. A spiritually defining time in her life was spent at L'Abri in Switzerland. Susan has been married to Mac for 37 years and they live in Brentwood, Tennessee. They have three adult sons and two grandchildren. Susan regularly organizes support efforts for overseas mission agencies, has launched a local financial ministry, works with educational initiatives and has an exuberant, entrepreneurial spirit. She loves reading, gardening, entertaining and often has the opportunity to exercise her gift of hospitality. She has been an active Realtor for almost 30 years and enjoys assisting people during major life transitions.